Practical Guide to the Operational Use of the RPD Machine Gun – 1st Edition

By Erik Lawrence

Copyright ©2014 Erik Lawrence

Erik Lawrence
www.vig-sec.com   erik@vig-sec.com

Printed and bound in the United States of America

First printing 2012
Second printing 2014

ISBN-10: 1-941998-17-8
ISBN-13: 978-1-941998-17-5
EBOOK – ISBN-13: 978-1-941998-35-9
LCCN: Not yet assigned

I0169328

ATTENTION US MILITARY UNITS, US GOVERNMENT AGENCIES AND PROFESSIONAL ORGANIZATIONS: Quantity discounts are available on bulk purchases of this book. Special books or book excerpts can also be created to fit specific needs. For information, please contact:

Erik Lawrence
www.vig-sec.com   erik@vig-sec.com

Firearms are potentially dangerous and must be handled responsibly by individuals. The technical information presented in this manual on the use of the RPD Machine Gun reflects the author's research, beliefs, and experiences. The information in this book is presented for academic study only. Neither the author nor the publisher assumes any responsibility for the use or misuse of information contained in this book.

SAFETY NOTICE
Before starting an inspection, ensure the weapon is cleared. Do not manipulate the trigger until the weapon has been cleared of all ammunition. Inspect the chamber to ensure that it is empty and no ammunition is present. Keep the weapon oriented in a safe direction when loading and handling.

AMMUNITION NOTICE- This weapon fires the 7.62x39mm Soviet, not the 7.62x51mm or 7.62x54R. Firing the incorrect ammunition will damage the weapon and possibly injure the operator/assistant operator.

Training should be received from knowledgeable and experienced operators on this particular weapons system. Vigilant Security Services, LLC provides this training and continually perfects its instruction with up-to-date information from actual use.

www.vig-sec.com

PREFACE

This manual is intended to be a reference for those involved in the use, maintenance, and instruction of the featured firearm. My aim in writing these manuals is to set the record straight and dispel many of the false assumptions related to the different firearms. The early sections of the manual contain background material on the featured firearm that allows the user to gain the basic building blocks for further education. The firearms featured in these manuals have been used for decades by our allies and enemies and will be for the foreseeable future, so why are we not experts with them? If I am fighting with a firearm or providing instruction on a firearm, I want to use and know its system better than my enemies do.

The rationale for writing these manuals comes from the fact that there are not libraries of easily accessible references to use in developing your own training system for these firearms. Many of the old military field manuals are decades old and were incorrectly translated by someone who had no idea what the firearm could do, let alone basic firearm knowledge. We started from the ground up and developed the manuals to provide instruction in progressive steps that could be easily grasped and to which the user could continually refer. A good grounding in the basics of firearms, safety, and instruction allows the user to use these manuals to their maximum value. A competent user will find little difficulty in interpreting and applying the information in the manual to one's own training program.

The guide goes through the most fundamental parts of the firearm in detail, and more advanced techniques are not covered as extensively. With this in mind, the user can use these principles and adapt them as needed to one's required level of instruction. The emphasis of this guide is in acquiring familiarity with the fundamentals of all firearms and learned competence rather than becoming a firearms guru.

Many of the points in these guides were developed from scratch in theatres of conflict and are continually improved and updated for each edition. I have continually used vetted points from users and professionals in the guides to update them constantly to the best-known practices for each particular firearm. If it is valid and relevant, we will include it in the next edition.

Please note that this guide assumes some familiarity with the basic concepts in firearm safety, gun handling skills, common sense, and an ability to process new information. Readers should have knowledge of the difference in calibers, countries of origin, and knowledge of the priority of the skills needed for development.

I hope you find this work useful and remember that a manual does not replace proper training and hands-on experience. Please email comments to erik@vig-sec.com, particularly if you find any errors or glaring omissions.

Table of Contents

Section 1 1
  Introduction 1
    Description.. 1
    Background.. 3
    Variants 4
    RPD Sights 8
    Zeroing the RPD-type LMG 9
    RPD - 7.62x39mm Ammunition 11

Section 2 15
  Maintenance... 15
  Clearing the RPD 20
    Disassembling the RPD 23
    Cleaning and Lubrication 30
    Inspecting the RPD 33
    Reassembling the RPD 34
    Performing a Function Check on the RPD MG 39

Section 3 40
  Operation and Function.. 40
    Loading the RPD Ammunition Belts... 40
    Loading the RPD 45
    Firing the RPD MG 48
    Cycle of Function 50

Section 4 53
  Performance Problems.. 53
    Malfunction and Immediate Action Procedures........................... 53

Appendix A – Ammunition Comparison 55
Appendix B – Munitions Packaging Markings 56
Appendix C – Weapon Identification Markings.............................. 59
Appendix D – Non-Standard Weapons Theory.............................. 61

1st Edition

Section 1

Introduction

The objective of this manual is to allow the reader to be able to use the RPD weapon system competently. The manual will give the reader background/specifications of the weapon and instruct on its operation, disassembly and assembly, proper firing procedure, and malfunction/misfire procedures. Operator-level maintenance will also be detailed to allow the reader to understand fully and become competent in the use and maintenance of the RPD Machine Gun.

Description

The **РПД**, **Р**учной **П**улемёт **Д**егтярёва, in Russian and **RPD,** *Ruchnoy Pulemyot Degtyaryova,* in English: meaning hand-held machine gun of Degtyaryov. The RPD is a 7.62mm light machine gun developed in the Soviet Union by Vasily Degtyaryov and the first light machine gun (LMG) to use an intermediate 7.62x39mm M43 cartridge. It is also sometimes called an RPD-44. It was created as a replacement for the DP machine gun chambered for the 7.62x54mmR round. It is a precursor of most squad automatic weapons and was issued to all infantry sections in the Soviet army up until 1961. It was replaced by the RPK, but many are still in Russian stockpiles.

The RPD is a belt-fed, air-cooled, open-bolt (full-automatic only) weapon using a gas-operated long-stroke piston system and a locking system recycled from previous Degtyaryov small arms, consisting of a pair of hinged flaps set in recesses on each side of the receiver. This is the same type of locking system found on the DShK, as Degtyaryov designed it also. The movement of these two horizontally pivoted locking flaps and the resulting locking and unlocking action is controlled by carefully angled surfaces on the bolt carrier assembly. The weapon fires from the open bolt, so as the trigger is pulled, the bolt carrier moves forward. As it moves forward, the locking flaps are pushed outwards by a vertical section of the bolt carrier which also strikes the firing pin once the bolt is fully locked into battery. Empty cases are ejected out the bottom of the receiver as on a DShK, and a spent shell deflector directs it to the right. This shell deflector also has rails to allow for the mounting of the ammunition drum.

It is fed from metallic-link belts; normally two coupled 50-round sections are carried in a drum-type belt container under the gun. The Chinese guns often use four 25-round sections. The RPD fires the 7.62x39-mm M1943 cartridge.

The gas system has a 3-positioned (1, 2, and 3) gas regulator for tuning the amount of gas introduced into the operating system. Older RPD models had shorter gas pistons and varied gas regulators in comparison to later models.

Unlike earlier Degtyaryov guns, the return spring is located inside the buttstock. The medium-weight barrel cannot be quick changed as it is screwed into the receiver and pinned into position. The RPD can still provide significant firepower at ranges up to 800 meters with a 300-rounds-a-minute sustained fire capability. Rear sights are standard open notch rear sights which are adjustable for range in 100-meter increments out to 1000m. The rear sight is also adjustable for windage. The front sight is a hooded post which can be adjusted for elevation when zeroing the weapon.

The folding integral bipod is located under the barrel and is not adjustable for height.

The RPD uses a single-stage belt feed; it uses a non-disintegrating link which has open links to allow the round to be pushed through the link and guided into the chamber once the trigger is pulled. The RPD was used as a squad automatic weapon that uses a detachable round box (drum) that is clipped under the receiver. This box can hold 100 rounds of non-disintegrating metallic belt; loose belts can also be used but with caution. The 100-round belt consisted of two 50-round link sections which can be connected with a round. Loose belts, not in the drum, violently whip during the firing of the weapon. Each belt drum has its own folding carrying handle, but usually belt drums are carried in canvas pouches.

The feed tray cover is hinged and can be opened to load and/or clear the weapon of ammunition. One of the two belt sections in the ammunition drum will have a flat steel lead tab so the weapon may be loaded without opening the cover.

The charging handle is on the right side of the rectangular receiver. There are two versions of the charging handle. The earlier models had one which was connected directly to the bolt carrier and reciprocated during firing. Later models utilized a separate non-reciprocating charging handle that could be folded up and out of the way.

This operator's manual will educate the reader as to basic operations and descriptions of this weapon system.

Background

During 1943, work on the weapon commenced, and three prominent Soviet engineers were tasked to submit their own designs: Vasily Degtyaryov, Sergei Simonov, and Alexei Sudayev. Among the completed prototypes prepared for evaluation, the Degtyaryov design proved superior and was accepted into service with the Soviet armed forces as the 7.62mm *Ручной Пулемёт Дегтярёва, РПД* (RPD, *Ruchnoy Pulemyot Degtyaryova* or "Degtyaryov light machine gun"), model 1944. Although the RPD was ready for mass production during the final stages of World War II, large-scale delivery of the weapon did not begin until 1953. During the Vietnam War, the RPD served the Viet Cong as their standard general-purpose machine gun. The RPD is a worldwide weapons system and will be seen in use and in caches for a long time. As with the AK rifle system, the RPD was distributed to all Soviet satellites and many terrorist groups during the Cold War to offset our arming of our allies.

After the introduction of the Kalashnikov-pattern support weapons such as the RPK and PK machine guns in the 1960s, the RPD was withdrawn from most first-tier units of the former Warsaw Pact. However, the RPD remains in active service in many African and Asian nations. Apart from the former Soviet Union, the weapon was manufactured in China -- Type 56 LMG, Egypt, Hungary RPD-74 made by FEG, North Korea -- Type 62, and since 1956, in Poland.

The RPD is a Degtyaryov-designed weapon, and its functions, with the exception of its belt-feed device, are almost exactly like the Degtyaryov DP light machinegun. The sole exception to the basic functioning lies in the locking action; the DP uses a cam on its firing pin to force the locking flaps into the locked position, whereas the RPD uses a cam machined in the slide. This cam also acts as a hammer to strike the firing pin; however, for all practical purposes, the hammer cam can be considered to function in the same way as the cam on the firing pin of the DP.

Variants

Modifications made to increase the operational reliability of the RPD have resulted in the following distinct versions:

1. First version: Cup-type gas piston, no dust cover; straight reciprocating handle, right-hand windage knob. Most first-version guns now have a cylinder sleeve fitted to the gas spigot so that their gas mechanism resembles the later versions and have a sliding dust cover fitted over the operating handle slot.

2. Second version: Plunger-type gas piston, no dust covers, straight reciprocating operating handle, left-hand windage knob. Some second-version guns have had a sliding dust cover similar to the ones fitted to the first-version guns; others have had a bracket riveted to the side of the receiver to accept a non-reciprocating operating handle. This latter type may have a handle that folds upward like the later model RPDs, or one that folds forward.

3. Third version: (also PRC Type 56) Like the second version, but has dust covers on feed mechanism and folding non-reciprocating operating handle.

4. Fourth version: Like the third version, but with a longer (RPDM) gas cylinder, additional roller on the piston slide, and buffer in butt.

5. Fifth version: (PRC Type 56-1) As the fourth version, but with a folding magazine bracket/dust cover and cleaning rod (sectional) carried in butt. These changes have no effect on the gun's operation and very little effect upon its functioning. The RPD has also been manufactured in the People's Republic of China as the Type 56 and Type 56-1 light machine guns and in North Korea as the Type 62 light machine gun. These latter types can be identified by the Chinese or Korean markings on their feed covers.

Russia – RPD LMG

Figure 1-1 Russian RPD LMG

A. Country of Origin: USSR/Russia

B. Military Designation: **RPD** (*Ruchnoy Pulemyot Degtyaryova*)

C. Cartridge Type: <u>7.62x39mm</u> cartridge

D. Type of Feed: Belt-fed

E. Locking System: Locking flaps

F. System of Operation: Gas operated

G. Range: Maximum effective range of 800m/880 yards

H. Weight:

    a. LMG – 7.4 kg/16 pounds, including the bipod
    b. LMG with loaded drum – 9 kg/19.8 pounds
    c. Loaded drum of 100 rounds – 1.6 kg/3.5 pounds

I. Length: 1,036 mm/40 inches

J. Length of barrel: 520 mm/20 inches

K. Belts: Metallic non-disintegrating, two 50-round link sections in round metal can

L. Rate of fire: 300 rounds/min

M. Muzzle velocity: 735 m/sec/2411 fps

China – Type 56 LMG

Figure 1-2 Chinese Type 56 LMG

Poland – RPD LMG

Figure 1-3 Polish RPD LMG (note the circled 11)

Figure 1-4 SOG Recon Team member firing a chopped-off RPD

Figure 1-5 Viet Cong with a RPD

RPD Sights

The notched rear-tangent iron sight is adjustable, each setting denoting hundreds of meters, Figure 1-6b. The front sight is post adjustable for elevation in the field, Figure 1-6a. Windage adjustment is done by the armory prior to issue. Sight tools are now available to let operators quickly zero the rifle to their shooting positions. The battle setting places the round within a few centimeters above or below the point of aim out to approximately 350 meters. This "point-blank range" setting allows the shooter to fire the gun at any close target without adjusting the sights. Longer settings are intended for area suppression. These settings mirror the Mosin-Nagant and SKS rifles and the AK-47–type firearms. This feature eased transition and simplified training. The RPD rear sight is graduated from 100m to 1000m, with 100m increments and 400m battle sight setting.

Figure 1-6a   **Figure 1-6b**
Photo of standard front and rear sights

Figure 1-7 Photo of standard sight alignment

Zeroing the RPD-type LMG

Zero procedure: Attempt to do this on a known distance range on a windless day from a solid bench rest.

RPD-type weapons have two adjustable sights. The front can be changed for elevation and windage. The rear sight is adjustable for elevation once the front sight is regulated. Zeroing elevation adjustments and windage adjustments are made using the front sight. The rear sight is set up for a battle sight zero setting and 1-10 (hundreds of meters increment) with the slider. The tangent rear sight has a slider that has pre-calibrated elevation adjustments for different ranges. With tangent sights, the rear sight is often used to adjust the elevation once calibrated, and the front to adjust the windage. Elevation is controlled by moving the slide in the up or down position.

The front sight consists of a rotating sight post. The front sight will allow you to adjust and calibrate for elevation by rotating the front sight pin up or down.

Elevation Note: If you wish to move your point of impact up, then you must rotate the sight down. If you wish your point of impact to go down, you must rotate the front sight pin up.

Windage Note: If you wish to change your windage, then you must drift the windage drum in the opposite direction desired. I strongly suggest that you purchase an AK sight tool; it makes drifting your front sight much easier.

Front Sight Note: Any changes you make on your front sight must be made in the opposite direction.

Establish Battle Zero

The following procedure will establish a zero at 16 meters (near) and 350 meters (far) for 7.62x39mm and the length of the RPD's 20-inch barrel. This procedure will be for establishing a battle zero and will also calibrate your range indicators on the rear tangent sight with the slider. For these two zeros, you will keep your rifle on the lowest slider setting, which has different characters to denote battle zero. Different countries mark this setting differently, but "П" is a Cyrillic P for *program* (zero) in Russian.

Establish Mechanical Zero
- Slide the spring-loaded slider down the tangent sight until the range scale П mark is aligned with the top of the slider.
- Load a single round into the chamber, fire, and then repeat to create a pattern.

- Carefully aim and fire each shot of a 5-shot group at a paper target set up at 16 meters. If your shots are not striking the point of aim, then adjust your sights.
- To raise the next shot group, rotate the front sight post in the down direction (clockwise).
- To lower the next shot group, rotate the front sight post in the up direction (counter-clockwise).
- To move the next shot group left, loosen the front sight cross bolt and screw and then drift the front sight to the right and retighten the bolt.
- To move the next shot group right, loosen the front sight cross bolt and screw and then drift the front sight to the left and retighten the bolt.
- Continue to fire 5-shot groups and adjust the sights until you have a tight group at the point of aim.
- Once you complete this step, the rifle is now combat-zeroed; all other ranges on the elevation scale are also zeroed, so to engage target at, say 500 meters, slide the spring-loaded slider to 5.
- Once the weapon is zeroed, you can set the slider on the battle sight zero for shooting from 0-400 meters without changing the elevation. While using a battle zero, you will have to remember your ballistics and adjust your hold if shooting the mid range. For example, if you are shooting at 200m, you will have to hold slightly lower as this is around the maximum ordnance (highest point in the bullet's arc). My rule is to hold for belt line at any mid range and squeeze the trigger.

RPD - 7.62x39mm Ammunition

The Soviet **7.62x39mm** rifle cartridge was designed during World War II and first used in the SKS carbine. The cartridge was influenced by the late-war German 7.92mm *Kurz* (*Kurz* meaning short in German). Shortly after the war, the world's most recognized assault rifle was designed for this cartridge: the AK-47. The cartridge remained the standard Soviet load until the 1970s and is still by far the most common intermediate rifle cartridge used around the world. Its replacement, the 5.45x39mm cartridge, is less powerful but longer ranged (due to its much higher velocity) and is more controllable in full-auto fire (due to the lower recoil). The change was a response to the NATO switch from the 7.62mm cartridge to 5.56x45mm NATO.

Ballistics
The RPD fires a 7.62x39mm round with a muzzle velocity of 735 m/sec/2411 fps. Cartridge case length is 38.6 mm. Projectile weight is normally 8g/123 grain. The RPD, with the 7.62x39mm cartridge, has a maximum effective range of around 700 meters. For comparison, the 7.62x54mm cartridge has a projectile of 9.6-12 g/148-185 grain (depending on the weapon) at a velocity of 818m/s (2,683 ft/s) for approximately 4,000 joules/2,950 ft-lb of energy.

The original Soviet bullets are boat-tail bullets with a copper-plated steel jacket, a large steel core, and some lead between the core and the jacket. The cartridge itself consists of a Berdan-primed, tapered steel case which seats the bullet and contains the powder charge. The taper makes it very easy to feed and extract the round since there is little contact with the chamber walls until the round is fully seated. This taper is what causes the AK-47 to have distinctively curved magazines. While the bullet design itself has gone through a few redesigns, the cartridge itself remains largely unchanged.

M43 Bullet Design
Although the new cartridge represented a great leap forward from previous designs, the initial bullet design was flawed. The complete solidity of the M43 projectile causes its only drawback—it is stable even in tissue and begins to yaw only after traversing nearly 30cm of tissue. This characteristic greatly reduces the wounding effectiveness of the projectile against humans. Dr. Martin Fackler noted that the wounds from the M43 round were comparable to that of a small handgun round using non-expanding bullets. Unless the round struck something vital, the wound was usually small and quick healing. Extremity hits were seen as nearly inconsequential.

M67 Bullet Design
In the 1960s, the Yugoslavians experimented with new bullet designs to produce a round with a superior wounding profile to the M43. The Yugoslavian-type rounds are known as M67 and incorporate an air gap inside the front of the bullet that shifts the center of gravity rearward, causing the bullet to destabilize nearly 17cm

earlier in tissue. This feature causes a pair of large stretch cavities at a depth likely to cause effective wound trauma. When the temporary stretch cavity intersects with the skin at the exit area, a larger exit wound will result, which takes longer to heal. Additionally, when the stretch cavity intersects a stiff organ, like the liver or a full bladder, it will cause damage to that organ.

However, without fragmentation, the wounding potential of M67 is mostly limited to the small permanent wound channel the bullet itself makes. While a fragmenting round (like the 5.56x45mm) might cause massive tissue trauma and blood loss (and thus rapid incapacitation) on a lung or abdominal hit, the M67 has a greater chance of merely wounding the target. Still, it is an enormous improvement over the M43 design.

Nearly all modern 7.62x39mm rounds of civilian or military manufacture are of the M67 variety—a simple boat tail FMJ round with a forward air cavity. Notable exceptions are the Ulyanovsk Machine Factory EM1 "match" (which substitutes a nipple for an air cavity and produces a single large temporary cavity in place of two small ones) and the Wolf 150 grain/9.7 gram soft point, which behaves much more like a traditional expanding hunting round. Nearly all jacketed hollow point rounds in 7.62x39mm are M67 rounds with a small hole in the front of the jacket—terminal ballistics are nearly identical to their fully jacketed brethren. They are a concession to various hunting laws that forbid FMJ rounds. Of all the tested JHP rounds, only Ulyanovsk EM3 hollow points seem to expand at all.

Chinese Steel Core
Chinese military-issue ammunition in this caliber is M43 style with a mild steel core and a thin jacket of copper or brass. Contrary to common belief, the use of steel was a cost-saving measure rather than one to increase the penetration. Additionally, mild steel is not sufficiently hard to grant unusual armor-penetrating capability. Despite this, Chinese ammunition is currently banned from importation in the U.S. because that there are 7.62x39mm caliber "handguns" (mostly Krinkov pistols and a few single-shot target pistols), and the ammunition is an "armor-piercing handgun round" under the U.S. federal legal definition of the word, which is based on materials and bullet design rather than on tested ability to penetrate armor.

Other Names for 7.62x39mm
On some occasions, this ammunition is referred to as 7.62mm Soviet, 7.62mm Warsaw Pact rounds, or 7.62mm ComBloc. It was also known in the United States as .30 Short Russian; the "Short" was to distinguish it from the older .30 Russian (7.62mm Russian), which was the 7.62x54mm.

Since approximately 1990, the 7.62x39mm cartridge has seen some use in hunting arms in the U.S. for hunting game up to the size of whitetail deer, as it is approximately as powerful as the American .30-30 Winchester round and has a similar ballistic profile. Large numbers of inexpensive imported semi-auto rifles, like the SKS and semi-auto AK-47 clones and variants, are available in this caliber, and the SKS is so inexpensive as to have begun displacing the .30-30 lever-action rifles as the new "poor person's deer rifle." Inexpensive imported 7.62x39mm ammunition is also widely available, though much of it is of the non-expanding type that may be illegal to use for hunting in some states. However, a number of American civilian manufacturers produce soft-tip rounds, suitable and legal for hunting.

The 7.62x39mm ammunition used by the AK/AKM is produced by Russia, former Soviet republics, China, and many different European countries. The 7.62x39mm cartridges will be encountered in both brass and steel cases; however, steel cases are more prolific. The 7.62mm is the diameter of the bullet, and 39mm is the length of the case.

The following is a brief list of the different types of ammunition and their uses:

- Steel-core ball – for use against light material targets, personnel, or during training. The steel-core ball weighs 122 grains. No tip markings.

- Tracer – for observation of fire, incendiary effects, and signaling and for use during training. Green-tipped marking and primer painted green denotes the green trace when fired.

- Armor piercing – for use against lightly armored targets where armor-piercing effects are desired. Black tipped marking. No photo available.

- Blank – for use during training when simulating live fire. If blanks are to be fired from the RPD LMG, a blank adapter must first be fitted to the muzzle, and a blank fire gas regulator must be installed. Without the blank adapter, insufficient gas pressure is generated to cycle the weapon properly.

Ammunition Identification

7.62x39mm examples

Figure 1-8   **Figure 1-9**   **Figure 1-10**   **Figure 1-11**   **Figure 1-12**
Ball   Ball   Tracer   Frangible   Soft Point

Caliber, mm	Case	Bullet type	Bullet, wt. Grain	Primer Type	Description
7.62x39	Bimetal	Bimetal	122	Berdan	Steel Core
7.62x39	Bimetal	Bimetal	122	Berdan	Steel Core
7.62x39	Bimetal	Tracer T-45M	122	Berdan	Tracer Bullet
7.62x39	Brass	Frangible	125	Boxer	Frangible
7.62x39	Brass	Soft Point	125	Boxer	Soft Point

Standards for small arms ammunition are given below.

Color	Type
None	Ball L (lead core)/Ball PS (steel core)
Yellow	Heavy Ball D
Yellow/Silver	Heavy Ball D (steel core)
Silver	Light Ball LPS (Steel core) - Obsolete
Green	Tracer
Black	AP
Black/Red	API
Black/Yellow	API - Obsolete
Purple	AP-T
Purple/Red	API-T
Red bullet with black tip	API (Carbide core)
Red/Red primer	HEI
Black/Green	Reduced velocity (Sub sonic)
Crimped extended case	Blank

Section 2

Maintenance

Figure 2-1 RPD Disassembled, complete

1- Receiver
2- Feed Tray Cover
3- Forearm
4- Gas Block
5- Barrel
6- Muzzle
7- Buttstock/Trigger Assembly
8- Gas Regulator and Gas Regulator Retention Bolt
9- Bolt Carrier/Piston Rod
10- Operating Rod
11- Operating Spring
12- Operating Spring Retainer
13- Charging Handle
14- Locking Flaps
15- Bolt
16- Trigger
17- Safety Lever
18- Ammo Can Hanger
19- Feed Tray
20- Sear
21- Gas Piston Tube
22- Gas Piston
23- Gas Regulator
24- Gas Regulator Retention
25- Combo Tool

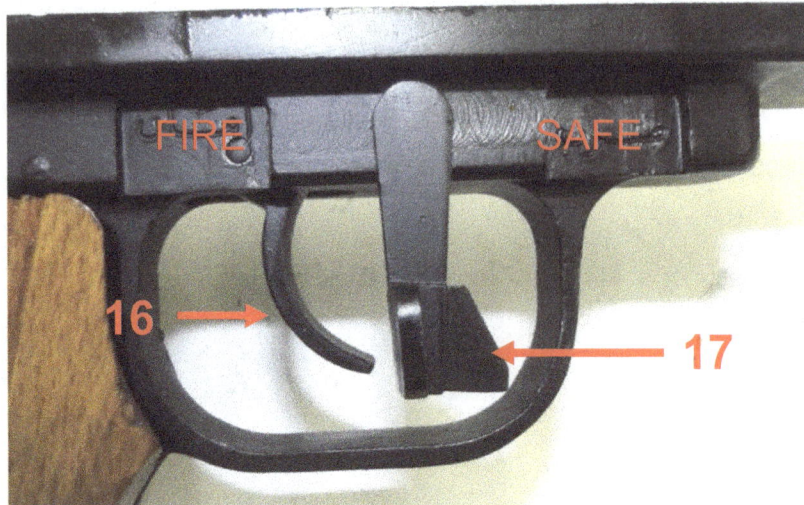

Figure 2-2 RPD Safety (safety in mid position for illustration)

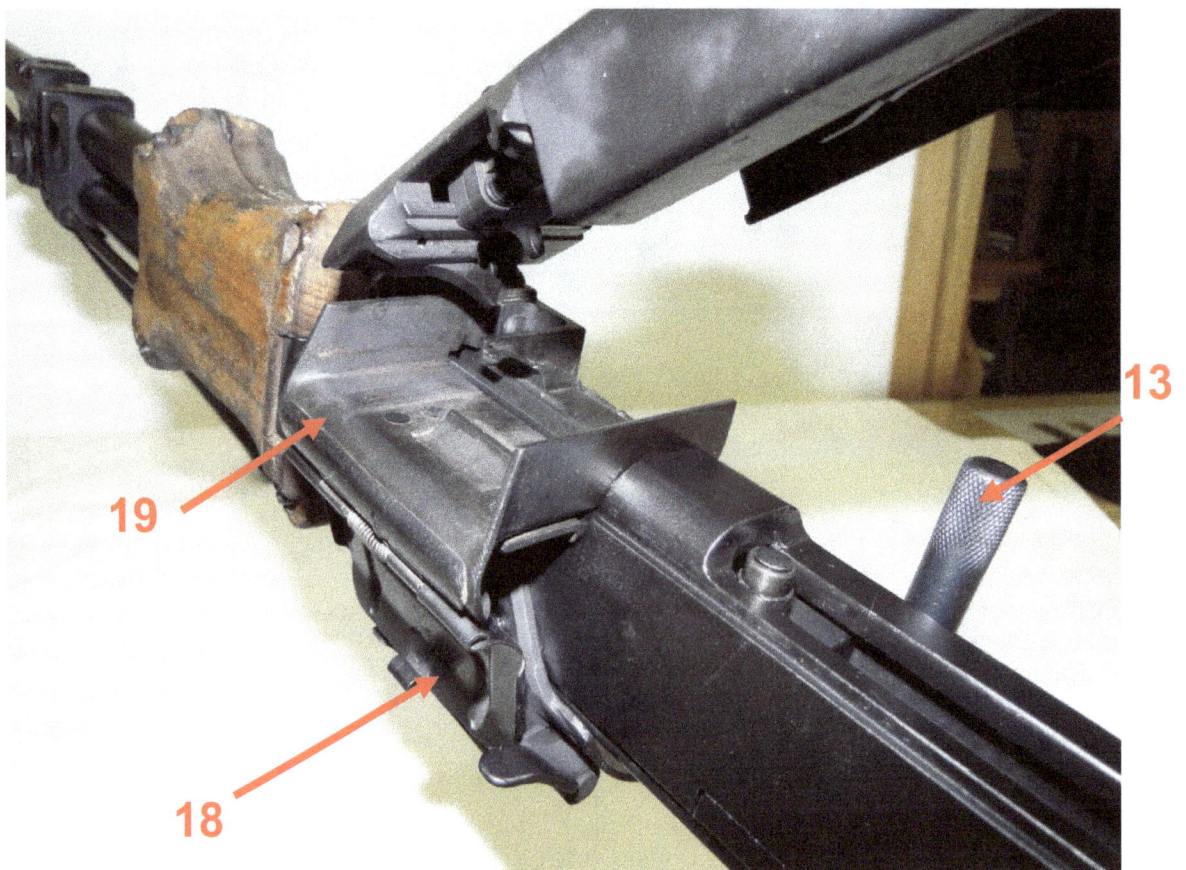

Figure 2-3 RPD Feed tray area of receiver

Figure 2-4 RPD Sear assembly

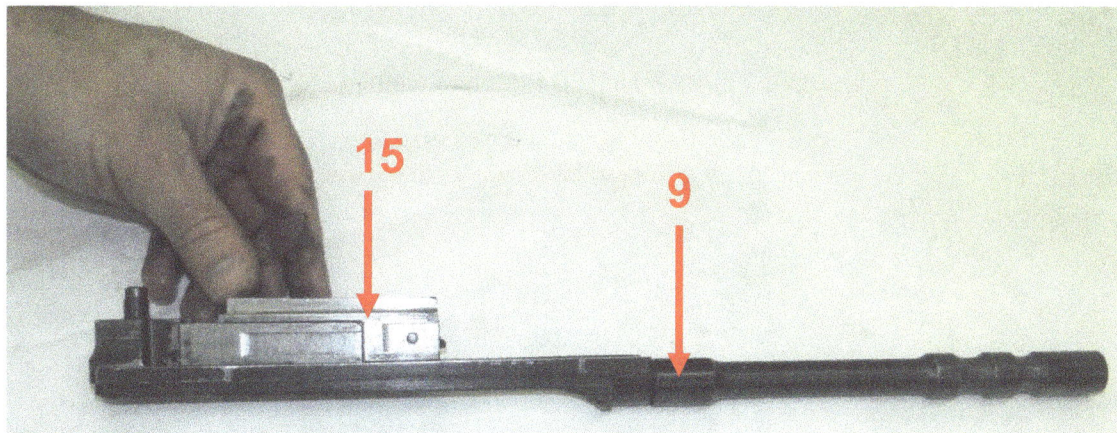

Figure 2-5 RPD Disassembled, slide assembly

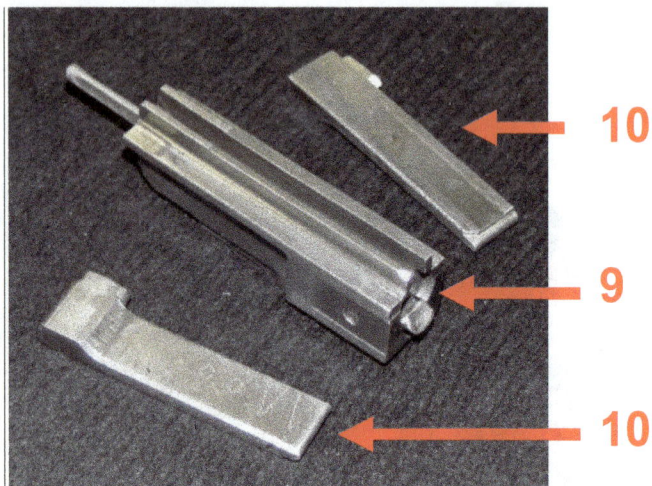

Figure 2-6 RPD Disassembled, bolt

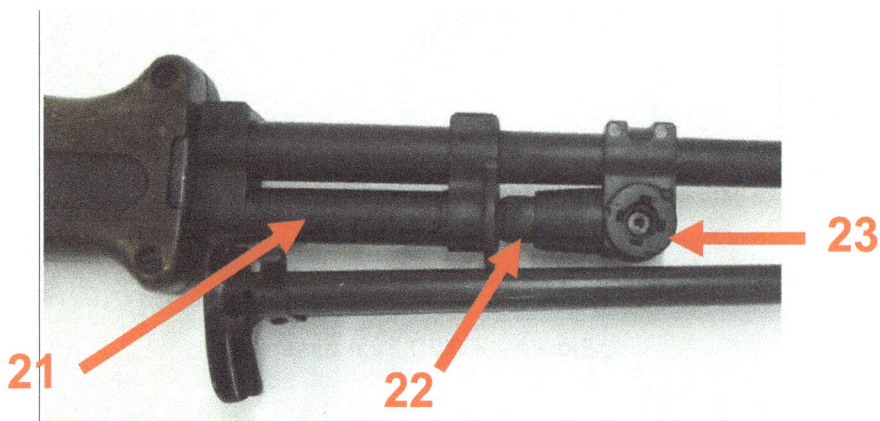

Figure 2-7a RPD Piston system

Figure 2-7b Gas regulator parts

1- Receiver
2- Feed Tray Cover
3- Forearm
4- Gas Block
5- Barrel
6- Muzzle
7- Buttstock/Trigger Assembly
8- Gas Regulator and Gas Regulator Retention Bolt
9- Bolt Carrier/Piston Rod
10- Operating Rod
11- Operating Spring
12- Operating Spring Retainer
13- Charging Handle
14- Locking Flaps
15- Bolt
16- Trigger
17- Safety Lever
18- Ammo Can Hanger
19- Feed Tray
20- Sear
21- Gas Piston Tube
22- Gas Piston
23- Gas Regulator
24- Gas Regulator Retention
25- Combo Tool

Clearing the RPD

Figure 2-8 Charging handle

A. Pull the bolt to the rear by the charging handle (Figure 2-8).

Figure 2-9 Safety lever

B. Place the weapon on "SAFE," safety lever forward (Figure 2-9).

Figure 2-10 Feed tray catch

C. Open the feed-tray cover by pushing the cover catch (Figure 2-10).

Figure 2-11 Remove ammunition belt

D. Lift up the feed-tray cover; remove any belt in the mechanism (Figure 2-11).

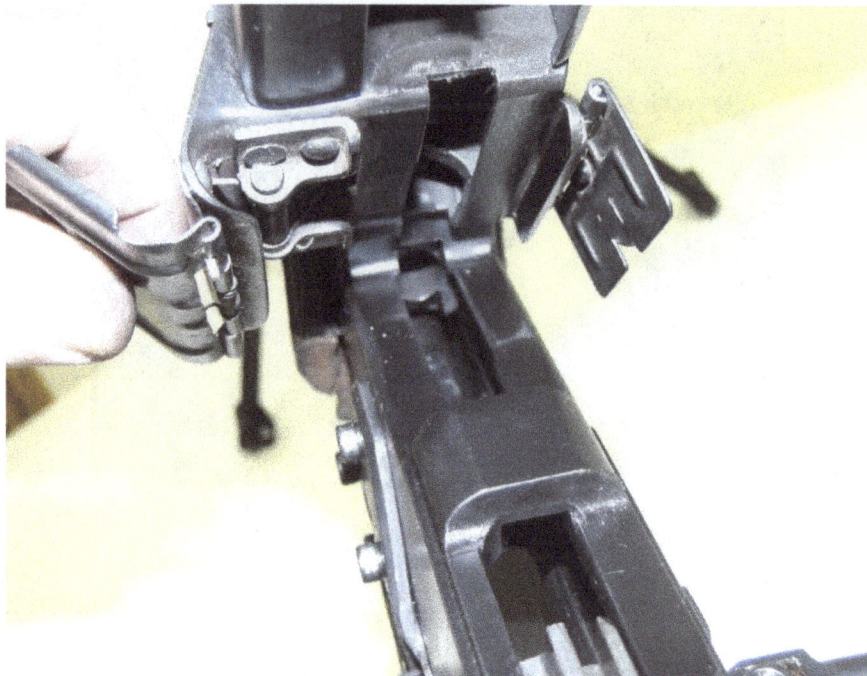

Figure 2-12 Lifting the feed tray to inspect the chamber

E. Lift up the feed tray; remove any round in the mechanism (Figure 2-12).

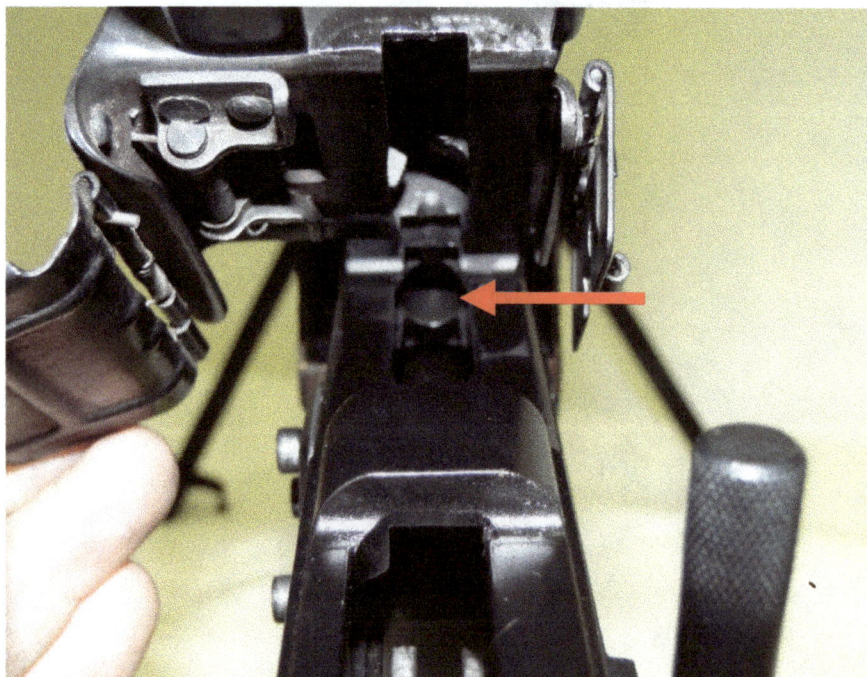

Figure 2-13 Inspecting the chamber

F. Inspect the face of the bolt and chamber to ensure it is clear of ammunition (Figure 2-13).

G. Rotate the safety to "FIRE" if on "SAFE".

Figure 2-14 Returning the bolt to the forward position, ride it forward

H. Holding the operating handle, press the trigger and ease the bolt forward (Figure 2-14); then place back on "SAFE."

I. Close the feed-tray and feed-tray cover.

Disassembling the RPD

NOTE: Place the weapon's parts on a flat, clean surface with the muzzle oriented in a safe direction.

To insure the proper function of the RPD, it is necessary to disassemble the weapon to inspect and clean the internal components. The names of the parts should be learned through practice in disassembling and reassembling to enhance operator competence. Generally the parts are named for the functions they perform, i.e., the trigger guard guards the trigger, the charging handle is used to charge the weapon, etc.

When the operator begins to disassemble the weapon, it should be done in the following order:

A. Ensure the weapon is clear, the weapon is off the "SAFE" position, the bolt and bolt carrier are forward, and the feed-tray cover and feed tray are open.

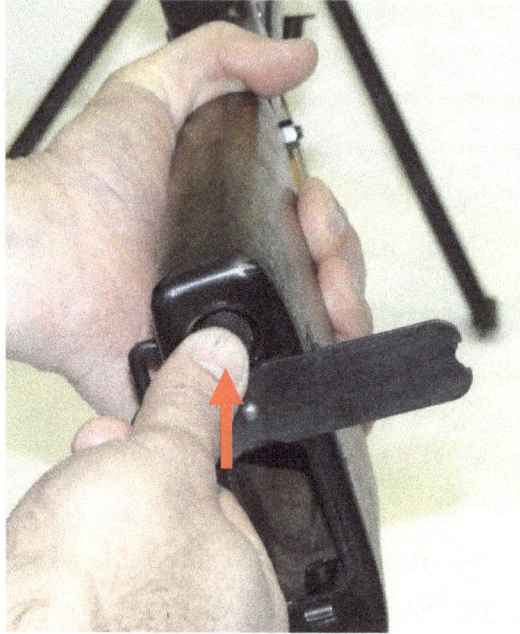

Figure 2-15a   **Figure 2-15b**
Unlocking the operating spring retainer

B. Pivot the plate on the buttstock to expose the operating spring retainer. This retainer is knurled and slotted. Press in and rotate the retainer to the left one quarter turn and while under control, bring the operating spring and rod out of the weapon (Figures 2-15a and b). Set the operating spring/rod assembly down.

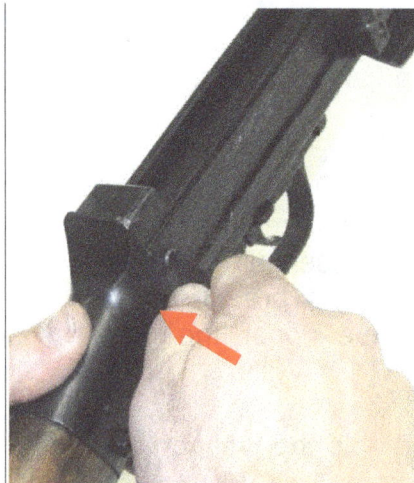

Figure 2-16a   **Figure 2-16b**
Removal of receiver retaining pin

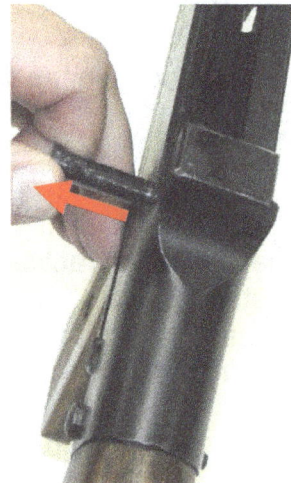

C. Push out the receiver retaining pin, from right to left as it is retained on the receiver and not removable, with a drift pin until it stops (Figures 2-16a and b).

Figure 2-17a   **Figure 2-17b**

Buttstock removal

D. Pull the buttstock rearward to remove it from the receiver and set it aside. If present, the cleaning rod will be removed at this time also (Figure 2-17a).

Figure 2-18a Bolt carrier removal

Figure 2-18b Bolt carrier and piston assembly

E. Remove the bolt carrier assembly by sliding it to the rear of the receiver by the charging handle (Figure 2-18a). Once the bolt carrier group is out of the receiver, you can now take the charging handle off by pulling it fully to the rear and lifting it out of the recessed cut.

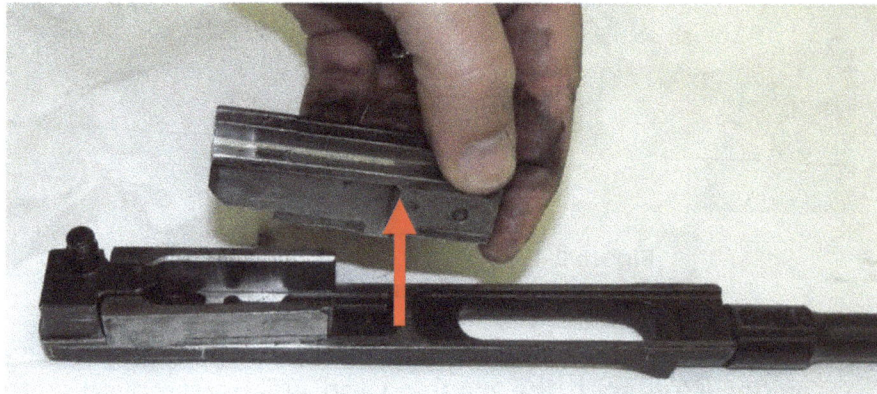

Figure 2-19 bolt assembly removal

F. Lift the bolt off the operating slide (Figure 2-19).

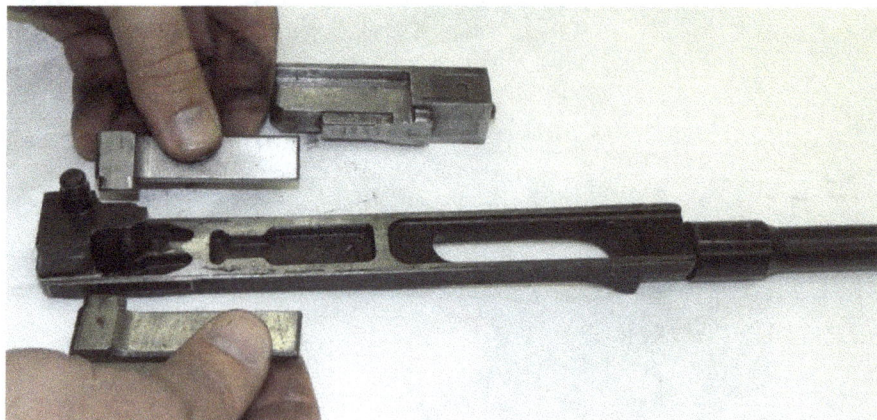

Figure 2-20 Locking flaps removal

G. Remove the locking flaps (Figure 2-20).

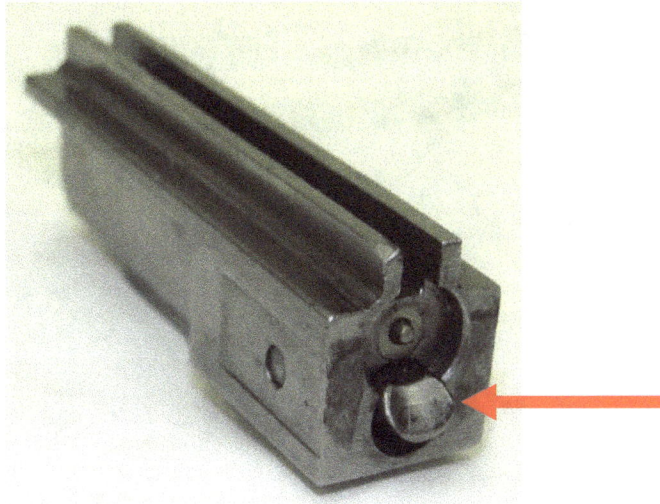

Figure 2-21 Extractor inspection

H. On the bolt face, inspect the extractor for chips, burrs, or lack of spring tension (Figure 2-21).

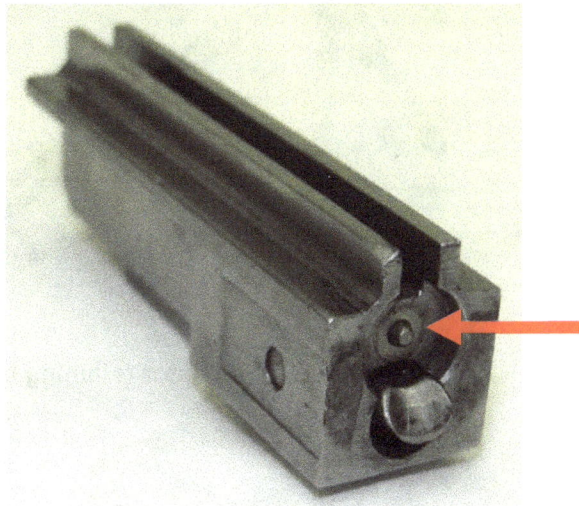

Figure 2-22 Firing pin inspection

I. On the bolt face, inspect the firing pin for chips and burrs, and that it freely floats in the bolt (Figure 2-22).

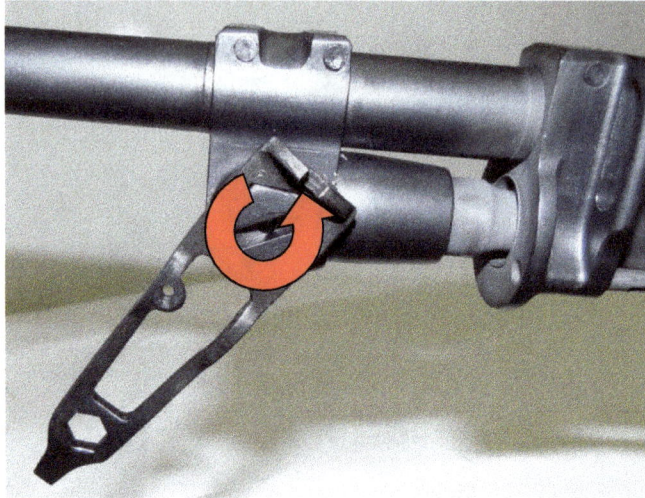

Figure 2-23a Gas regulator retaining bolt loosening

Figure 2-23b Gas regulator retaining bolt removal

Figure 2-23c Gas regulator removal from the gas block

Figure 2-23d Gas regulator removal

J. Use the combo tool to loosen the gas regulator retaining bolt by turning it left until it is removed (Figure 2-23a). Once it is fully out (Figure 2-23b), push the gas regulator to the right through the gas block to separate it from the barrel (Figure 2-23c). NOTE: the three settings of the gas regulator are denoted by a "1," "2," and "3" (Figure 2-23d). Replacing the regulator with the number nearest the post will allow for the amount of gas selected. The higher the number, the more gas, and the faster it will operate.

Figure 2-24 Sear assembly inspection

K. Inspect the sear for damage – chipped or cracked sear. Check the spring tension of the safety disconnect while checking the SAFE/FIRE function (Figure 2-24).

Figure 2-25 Operator-level disassembled weapon

Cleaning and Lubrication

The RPD is a very dependable machine gun, but periodic cleaning is advised to insure functionality. Clean the weapon as often as the situation dictates and the environment necessitates.

Keep the weapon free of dirt and dust as much as possible; use a muzzle cap or tape to keep them from the bore. Depending on the operating environment, keep lubricant only on metal-to-metal moving parts and use paint brushes to clean dust and dirt off of and out of the weapon.

Do not clean the inside of the gas piston cover unless you have fired blanks or it is excessively sluggish, induced by carbon build-up. Do not put lubricants in the gas piston cover.

In hot and humid climates, inspect the weapon often for signs of rust. Keep the weapon free of moisture and keep a fine coat of lubricating oil on the metal surfaces. If the weapon is exposed to salt air, high humidity, or water, then clean and oil the weapon entirely as often as needed to keep it serviceable.

In hot and dry climates such as deserts, keep the weapon lubricated only on metal-to-metal moving parts and use paint brushes to clean dust and dirt off of and out of the weapon. Keeping the weapon free of unneeded oil will prevent sand and dust from collecting in the receiver and bore.

Keep your ammunition in containers and the canvas carriers when not in use and clean off the cartridges as necessary.

Clean the barrel with the cleaning rod that is stored on the left side of the machine gun and the brushes and jags stored in the hollow section of the buttstock. Use solvent-lubricated brass brushes to break up carbon in the bore, a solvent-covered patch to push the carbon out, and then a dry patch until it is clean. The bores are chrome lined, so they clean up easily. Keep spare barrels clean by taping the chamber and muzzle, storing them in the spare barrel bags, and inspecting them regularly. A boresnake is a great bore-cleaning product to use as the barrel is clean with one pass of the bore snake. Bore snake for the 7.62 caliber is item number VSS-240115.

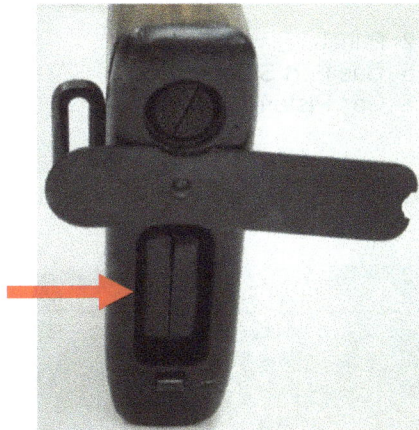

Figure 2-26 Maintenance kit stored in the buttstock

The RPD maintenance kit, which is stored in the buttstock (Figure 2-26), has specialized tools just for cleaning the RPD (Figures 2-27a and 2-27b). There are scrapers for the gas port, piston face, etc. Inventory these tools, and when there is a critical or hard-to-clean spot, it is probably done by a tool in the kit.

Figure 2-27a Tools and scrapers in the maintenance kit

1- Combination Tool   2- Punch   3- Cleaning Patch Jag
4- Steel Rod   5- Gas Port Scraper   6- Firing Pin
7- Ruptured Case Extractor   8- Gas Piston Scraper   9- Front Sight Wrench
10- Extractor

NOTE: Not pictured is a spare extractor spring with comes in the kit.

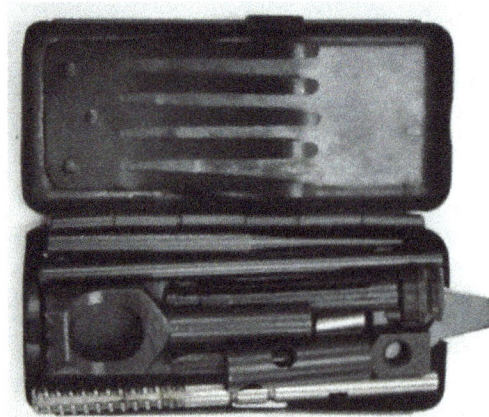

Figure 2-27b Tools in the maintenance kit ready for storage

Lubrication

Lube all operating parts where metal contacts metal and move. Inside the receiver, go ahead and coat the metal in a light film of CLP or light machine/gun oil. Some type of grease can be used on the metal-to-metal contacts (shiny spots) to allow the rifle to operate smoothly.

Inspecting the RPD

To insure an RPD is serviceable and ready for action, it needs to be inspected periodically and between firings. This inspection can take place while the operator is cleaning the weapon. Disassemble as per the previous section and organize the parts in groups to be inspected.

Parts to inspect: The overall condition of the weapon and components

Individual parts-
- The firing pin should be inspected for wear or breakage on the tip.
- The operating spring and guide rod should be inspected to insure they have not been chipped, bent, or broken.
- The extractor should be checked to see that it is under spring tension and is not chipped or worn.
- The trigger housing group should no show signs of excessive wear. All barrels should be inspected for cracks, burrs, and/or bends.
- The gas-piston cover should be inspected to see if it has any dents that would impede the movement of the gas piston during firing.
- The gas regulator needs to be inspected to insure it is not too covered with carbon to prevent adjustment.

Reassembling the RPD

A. Reinsert the gas regulator by sliding it from the right side through the gas block. There are three gas settings for this weapon, numbered 1, 2, and 3 (the higher the number, the more gas introduced into the system). This regulator should be set to the lowest gas setting that will allow it still to function reliably.

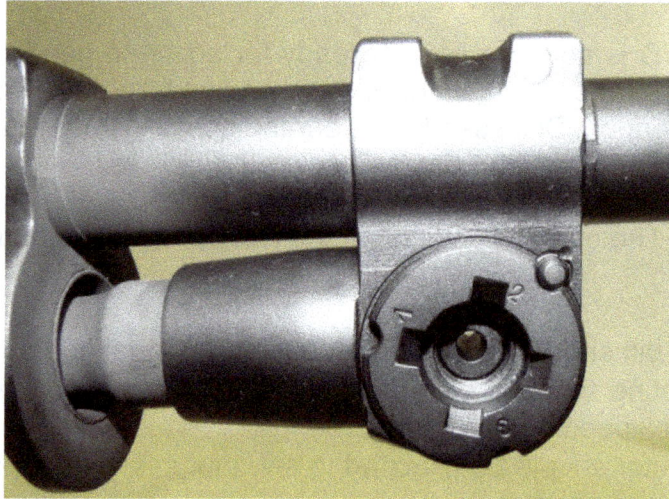

Figure 2-28 Gas regulator settings (photo shows the weapon on setting 2)

B. Align the appropriate number on the gas regulator with the post on the gas block when reinstalling the gas regulator (Figure 2-28).

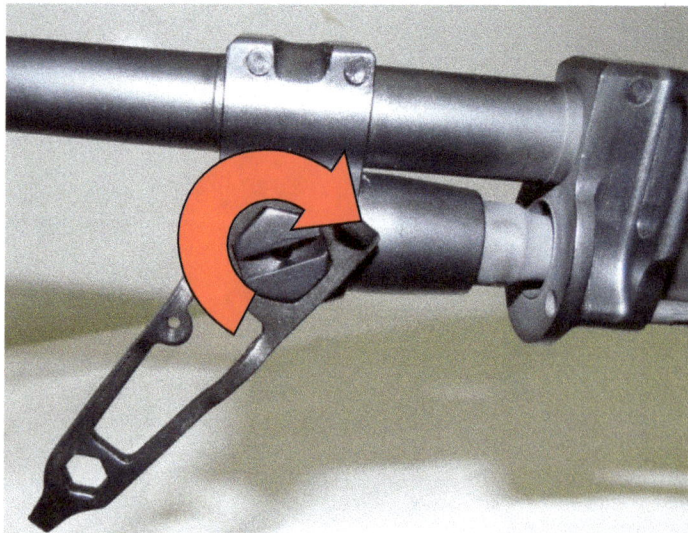

Figure 2-29 Gas regulator retention bolt installation

C. Start and tighten the gas regulator retention bolt; do not over tighten with the combo tool (Figure 2-29).

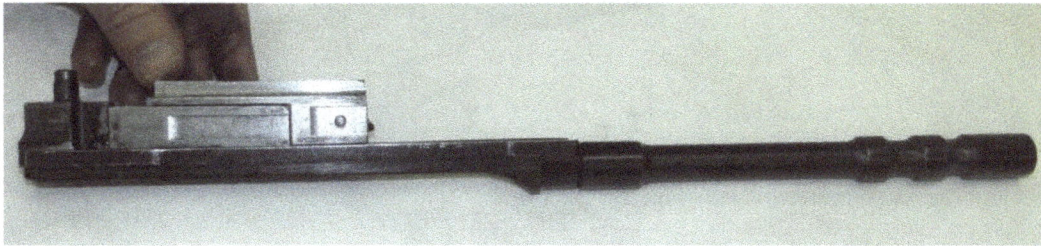

Figure 2-30 Bolt assembly

D. Realign the locking flaps onto the bolt and set the bolt onto the bolt carrier. Maintain an orientation so that the extractor is to the bottom (Figure 2-30).

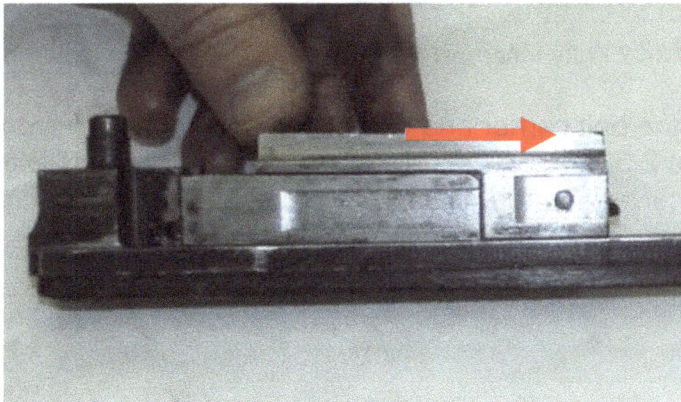

Figure 2-31 Bolt assembly onto slide

E. Push the bolt assembly forward on the slide until the locking flaps lie flush against the bolt (Figure 2-31).

F. Align the charging handle into the receiver recess and slide it forward.

Figure 2-32 Fully inserting the bolt carrier and piston assembly in receiver

G. Insert the bolt carrier and gas-piston assembly forward into the receiver (Figure 2-32). Align the rails of the carrier assembly with the grooves of the receiver. On the rear of the receiver, ensure the cross pin is pulled out to the left for the next step.

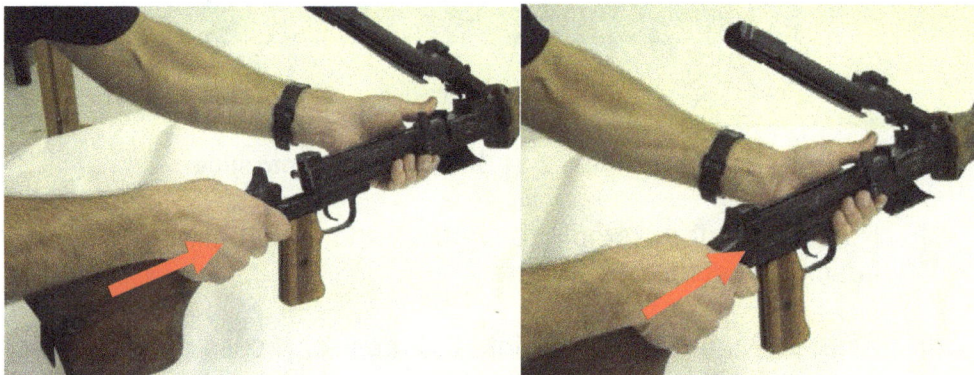

Figure 2-33a　　　　　　　　　　　**Figure 2-33b**
Buttstock reassembly

H. Slide the buttstock onto the receiver; slide the cleaning rod under the ammunition drum hanger and into the hole in the forearm. As you slide the buttstock on, guide the rear of the cleaning rod into the recess in the buttstock (Figures 2-33a and 2-33b).

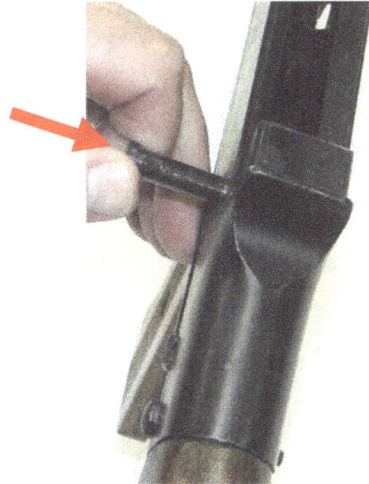

Figure 2-34 Press in the cross pin

I. Hold forward pressure on the buttstock until it stops and then press the cross pin in to the right to secure the two receivers (Figure 2-34).

Figure 2-35 Operating rod assembly installation

J. From the back of the buttstock, start the operating rod/spring assembly into the top hole. Once it is in, you must ensure the operating rod is seated into the rear hole on the bolt so as not to bend the rod during a function check (Figure 2-35).

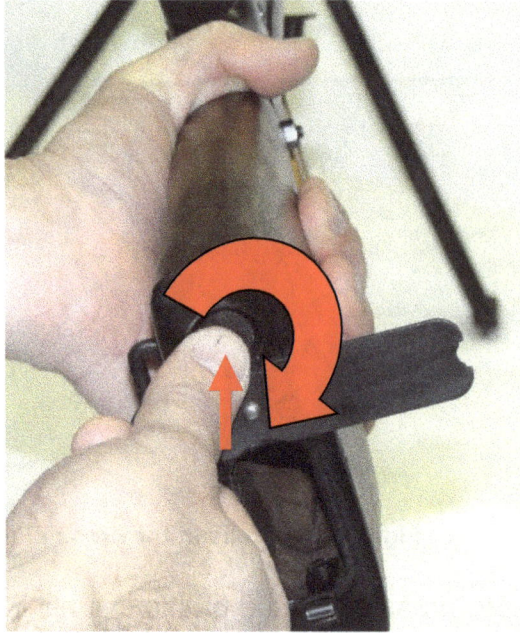

Figure 2-36 Securing the operating rod assembly

K. Turn the rear of the operating rod/spring assembly to the right while holding forward pressure; you may need to use a screwdriver or the combo tool to do this (Figure 2-36).

L. Close the feed tray and feed-tray cover.

Performing a Function Check on the RPD MG

A. Ensure the weapon is clear of any ammunition and the safety is on "FIRE".

B. Pull the operating handle until the bolt locks to the rear.

C. Rotate the safety forward to the "SAFE" position.

D. Pull the trigger; bolt should not go forward.

E. Rotate the safety rearward "FIRE."

F. Hold the charging handle to the rear and pull trigger. The bolt should be released forward; do this step gently and do not let it slam onto an empty chamber.

G. With the trigger held to the rear, cycle the action; then let off the trigger to check if the sear will catch the bolt carrier in the rearward position.

H. If the sear catches when the trigger is released, then the gun is OK for use.

I. Ride the bolt back forward with the charging handle and place the weapon on "SAFE".

Section 3

Operation and Function

Loading the RPD Ammunition Belts

Ensure the belts are clean, rust-free, and without damage. Observe basic safety precautions of handling small arms ammunition at all times.

A. Ensure you have 7.62x39mm; this ammunition is easily confused with with 7.62x51mm NATO (.308 Winchester). Inspect it for uniformity, cleanliness, and serviceability. Check all for undented primers and use only issued ammunition.

Figure 3-1a   **Figure 3-1b**
Two types of RPD ammunition belts

A. Press the link down onto the cartridge to be loaded and align the rear of the casing by sliding it into position, depending on which link is to be used. Note in the above photos the difference and load (Figures 3-1a and 3-1b).

Figure 3-2a   **Figure 3-2b**
Two types of RPD ammunition belts

B. Connecting the two 50-round belt sections together depends on which type of link you have (Figures 3-2a and 3-2b). Above are the two different types, and it must be noted that you cannot link unmatched link sections together. With a matched pair, you can align the two link sections and insert a cartridge to hold them together.

Loading the link into the drum and onto the weapon

Figure 3-3a   **Figure 3-3b**
Opening up the RPD ammunition can

A. Use of the drum is much suggested as the belt is very violent during firing. The spring-loaded lid holds the round in the drum until it is drawn into the weapon. Unlock the lever on the drum so the rear of the magazine can be opened (Figures 3-3a and 3-3b).

Figure 3-4 100-round loaded belt ready to put into the can

B. Start with the end of the loaded belt which does not have the starter tab. Roll up the belt on itself until you are at the starter tab and ready to put it in the drum.

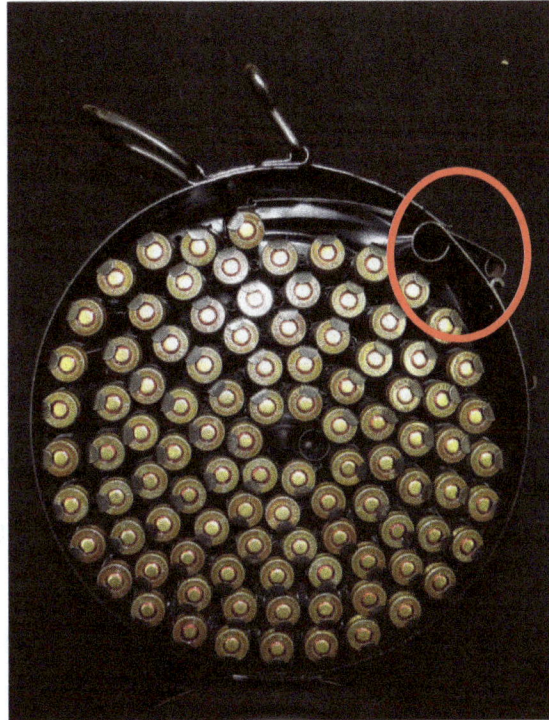

Figure 3-5 100-round loaded belt in the drum

C. Place the roll of link into the can with the starter tab through the spring-loaded door (Figure 3-5).

Figure 3-6 Loaded and ready ammunition drum

D. Close the back cover and lock the tab back down (Figure 3-6).

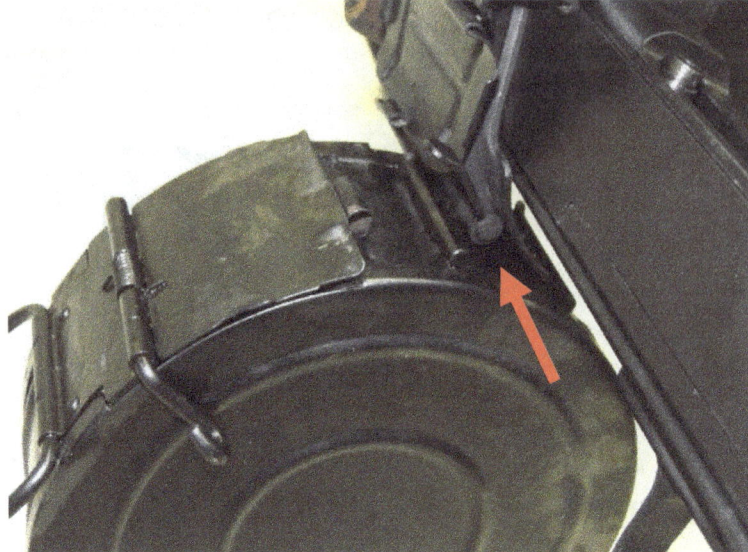

Figure 3-7 Sliding the ammo can onto the receiver

E. To place the drum on the weapon, align the can with the can hanger on the left side of the receiver (Figure 3-7).

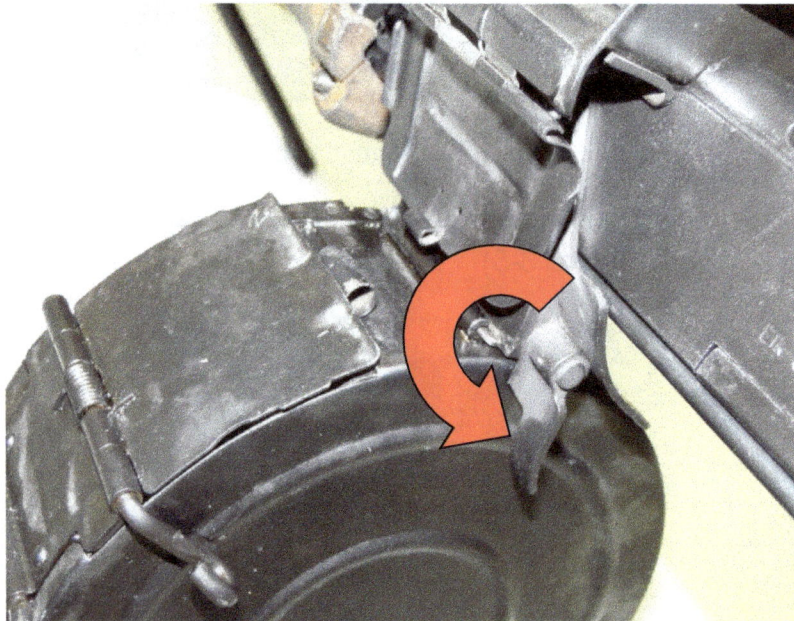

Figure 3-8 Rotating the can retainer down

F. Once the can is fully forward onto the can hanger, rotate the ammunition can retainer down to hold the can (Figure 3-8).

Loading the RPD

A. Clear the weapon as described previously and leave the feed-tray cover open, bolt forward, and weapon on FIRE.

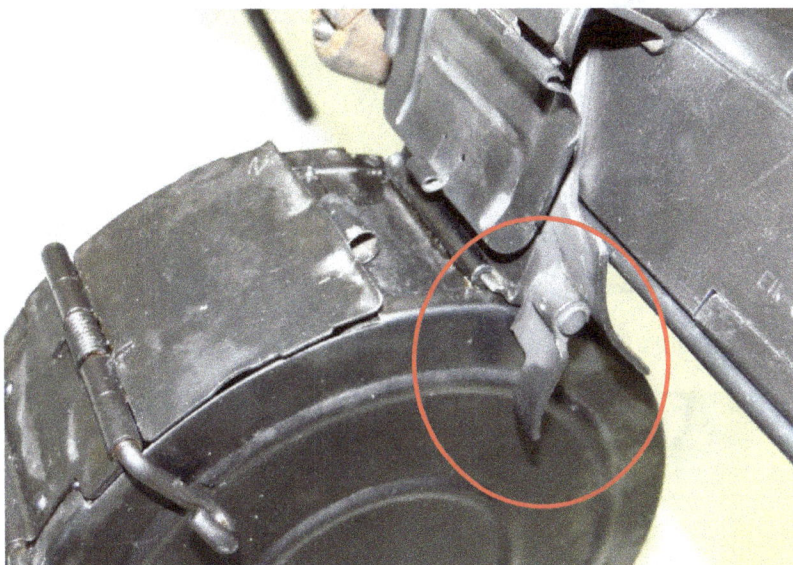

Figure 3-9 Locked-on ammunition can

B. Lock a can of ammunition onto the gun, turning the keeper latch up, and slide the drum onto the rails on the receiver. Once the drum is fully forward, rotate the keeper latch down into its locked position (Figure 3-9).

Figure 3-10 Inserting the starter tab on the RPD

C. If necessary, open the dust covers by opening and closing the feed cover. Then insert the lead tab of the belt into the feedway from left to right, and give it a vigorous pull to the right to seat the first cartridge in the holding pawl (Figure 3-10).

Figure 3-11a Pulling the charging handle to the rear

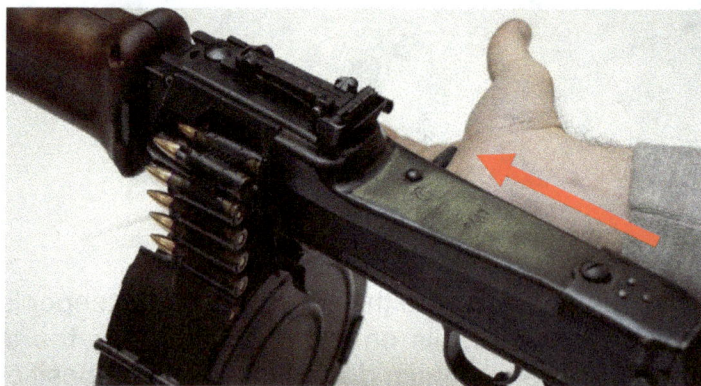

Figure 3-11b Returning the charging handle forward

Figure 3-11c Folding the charging handle up

D. Pull the operating handle to the rear (Figure 3-11a) until the bolt carrier is caught by the sear, unfolding the charging handle first, pulling it fully to the rear, and returning it forward (Figure 3-11b) on a third or later version RPD, then refolding it back up (Figure 3-11c).

Figure 3-12 Open feed cover loading

E. An alternative method of loading is to press the cover catch forward and open the cover. Pull the operating handle rearward, place the weapon on "SAFE", and lay a belt in the feedway with a cartridge in the feed lips (Figure 3-12). Close the feed tray cover.

Figure 3-13 Ammunition belt held in the loaded position

F. Hold the belt in place and shut the feed tray cover (Figure 3-13).

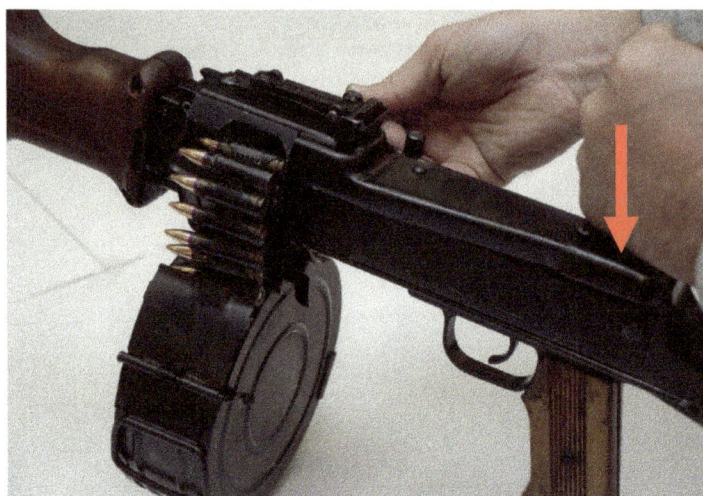

Figure 3-14 Closing the feed tray cover

G. When you shut the feed tray cover, pay attention to keep the rounds from sliding back out of the feed tray (Figure 3-14).

Firing the RPD MG

A. Prepare the weapon for firing by lubricating it. Motor oil (30-40 weight) made for high pressures and high temperatures is what is needed and is viscous enough to stick. Synthetic oil, if you can find it, is even better. Apply it on the feed tray to ensure it is dragged into the chamber and working parts as you fire.

C. Orient downrange or towards the threat; set your sight to the estimated range to target.

Figure 3-15 FIRE position for RPD safety lever

D. Push down and rotate the safety lever to the rear ("FIRE" position) (Figure 3-15).

E. Orient your sights onto the target, estimate the range, and adjust the rear sight to that estimate if needed. Maintain proper sight alignment and sight placement on the target.

F. Firmly slap the trigger to the rear and hold the trigger straight back and try not interrupt the sight picture. When you release, do it all at one time, not slowly. As the weapon has slight recoil, ensure the shooting position and/or mounting system is as tight as possible to allow for a reasonable beaten zone of impact, i.e., sandbagged. Do not "press or milk the trigger" as this action will cause malfunctions and damage the sear.

G. Maintain a 6- to 10-round bursts, and once your beaten zone is on the designated target, fire until you are happy with the results.

Figure 3-16 "SAFE" position for RPD safety lever

H. When you have completed firing the machine gun, place the safety lever into the "SAFE" position (forward) (Figure 3-16). Typically, if you have been firing at the enemy, not a target on a range, you should move.

Cycle of Function

Shooters can recognize and correct stoppages when they know how the RPD machine gun functions. Each time a round is fired, the parts of the weapon function in a cycle or sequence. Many of the actions occur at the same time.

These actions are separated in this manual only for instructional purposes.

1. The sequence of functioning is as follows:

    A. Feed
    B. Chamber
    C. Lock
    D. Fire
    E. Unlock
    F. Extract
    G. Eject
    H. Cock

2. The full-automatic cycle is started when the trigger is pulled. The sear is lowered down, releasing the bolt carrier. The locking flaps lock into battery as the carrier advances and drives the firing pin into the primer of the cartridge that was stripped from the ammunition belt. After firing, the bolt carrier moves to the rear, unlocking the locking flaps. As the weapon completes its cycle, the spring tension returns the bolt carrier forward to strip another cartridge from the belt. This cycle continues until the trigger is released or the ammunition supply is exhausted.

3. The RPD is a Degtyaryov-designed weapon, and its functions, with the exception of its belt-feed device, are almost exactly like the Degtyaryov DP light machine gun. The sole exception to the basic functioning lies in the locking action; the DP uses a cam on its firing pin to force the locking flaps into the locked position, whereas the RPD uses a cam machined in the slide. This cam also acts as a hammer to strike the firing pin; however, for all practical purposes, the hammer cam can be considered to function in the same way as the cam on the firing pin of the DP.

4. The belt feed is operated by the recoil and counter recoil of the slide. A feed roller on the top of the slide fits into the feed actuator lever, and as the slide moves rearward and forward, it causes this lever to move from side to side. The belt feed lever is pivoted to the middle of the feed cover and is driven by the actuator lever. The front end of the belt feed lever engages the feed slide. The movement of the slide is thus transmitted through the feed actuator lever and belt feed lever to provide the in-and-out motion of the feed slide that is required to move the feed belt into the gun. A stationary

spring-loaded belt holding pawl retains the belt in the gun as the feed slide moves in and out.

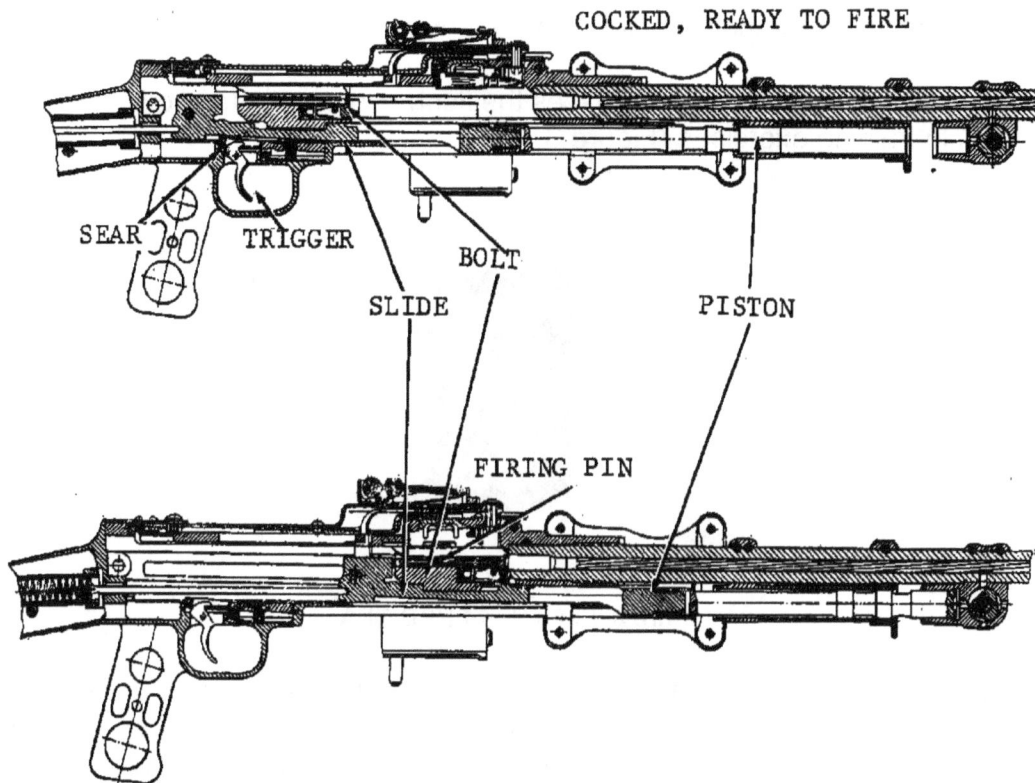

Figure 3-17 Top figure, ready to fire; bottom figure, at the instant of firing

Firing blanks from the RPD Machine Gun

To blank fire the RPD, you must remove the flash suppressor/muzzle break and replace it with the appropriate blank firing adapter

The Blank Firing Adapter (BFA) replaces the flash suppressor to allow for the firing of blanks in training exercises (Figure 3-18).

Figure 3-18 Photo of RPD BFA

To install, ensure the weapon is clear. Depress the spring-loaded detent and unscrew the muzzle protector. Then screw the adapter on and depress the spring-loaded detent until tight and release the detent to fit one of the cutouts on the adapter.

After blank fire, thoroughly clean all parts of the weapon which have had powder fouling as this is very corrosive to untreated metal.

Section 4

Performance Problems

Malfunction and Immediate Action Procedures

Malfunctions are usually preventable through good practices, but they may still occur out of the blue from time to time. Of course, you hope it is on the practice range, but you should treat each one as if you are in a life-or-death situation. Practicing proper and effective corrective actions will allow you to be more confident in your weapon handling. In stressful situations, you can become much more stressed due to an unforeseen malfunction that can be dealt with easily.

Proper training will do more to save your life than technology. Malfunction drills must fix the problem 100% of the time (excluding a weapon stoppage—broken weapon) the first time performed. You must look at the weapon and identify the problem (obviously the weapon is not functioning as you need it to, so you must transition to another weapon or rectify the situation). It is a non-functioning weapon at this point—fix it.

FAILURE TO FIRE This malfunction occurs when the belt has loaded a dud cartridge, the belt was not advanced far enough during loading, or you don't have a bolt in the weapon.

SYMPTOM - You pull the trigger to the rear, and you hear the bolt slam into the chamber with no round firing. This can also happen in the firing of a burst, but the symptom is the same.

    A.   **RACK-** The universal fix for this is to recharge the weapon (by pulling the charging handle to the rear and returning it forward) and watch for an unfired round to be ejected; maintain muzzle to threat orientation.

    B.   **BANG-** Attempt to refire. If it does not refire, move to the failure-to-feed malfunction corrective actions.

FAILURE TO FEED If weapon does not refire after a failure to fire that was recharged, then you must pull the bolt to the rear, place the weapon on SAFE, open the feed-tray cover, and re-lay your ammunition belt. As you are doing this step, look for any cartridges or casings in the action and/or chamber. Once you have re-laid your ammunition belt, close the cover. If you are to attempt to fire again, place the weapon on "FIRE", sight at the target, and attempt to engage.

NOTE: If the primer of the cartridge has been struck, then the ammunition is probably at fault; if the primer of the cartridge has not been struck, then the weapon is probably at fault.

FAILURE TO EXTRACT This malfunction is very common with the RPD and is the most time consuming to correct. This malfunction is created when the spent casing is not extracted from the chamber (due to faulty sized/manufactured ammo, dirty ammo, or a pitted chamber) and the next round to be loaded is rammed from the magazine into the rear of the stuck casing. Below is the breakdown of the corrective action to restore your weapon to operation.

> **STEP ONE**- With your finger off the trigger, pull the charging handle back to lock the bolt to the rear, and place the weapon on "SAFE".

> **STEP TWO**- Open the feed-tray cover; remove any ammunition belts and loose ammunition from the feed tray.

> **STEP THREE**- Lift the feed tray and inspect the chamber and receiver for casings. The casing that was not extracted will be seen still seated in the chamber.

> **STEP FOUR**- Either you or your assistant gunner needs to take the steel cleaning rod off of the weapon. Slide the rod down the bore from the muzzle end until it contacts the stuck casing. With a hammer, tap the rod until the casing is driven out of the chamber. Once the casing is out of the chamber, remove the steel rod from the muzzle and perform a normal loading procedure and attempt to refire. If time permits, clean the chamber and ensure your ammunition belts are clean and free of dirt.

Finally, it comes down to maintenance. Most of the ammo that is shot is poor quality; you are not supposed to fire captured ammo, but the reality of it is that it gets in the supply chain from time to time. The captured ammo has corrosive primers and will pockmark the chamber, causing the failure-to-extract malfunction, which is the most common complaint with the RPD. DO NOT FIRE ANY CAPTURED AMMUNITION! Inspect your chamber on all barrels as the more pitted they are, the more casing will stick on extraction. And yes, you should check the headspace of the barrel with the gauges and see if the weapon is safe to fire or is worn out.

Appendix A - Ammunition Comparison

| 9x18mm Makarov | 9x19mm Luger | 7.62x25mm Tokarev | .45 ACP |

PISTOLS AND SUBMACHINE GUNS

Size Comparison of NATO vs. Non-Standard Ammunition

| 5.56x 45mm | 5.45x 39mm | 5.56x 45mm | 7.62x 39mm | 7.62x 51mm | 7.62x 54R mm | 12.7x 99mm | 12.7x 108mm |

ASSAULT RIFLES   SNIPER RIFLES & MACHINE GUNS

Appendix B - Non-Standard Ammunition Packaging & Markings

Packaging

Russian small arms cartridges are packed in sealed sheet-metal containers, with two containers per wooden crate. Older Russian production used rectangular containers of heavy gauge galvanized iron with soldered seams. Around 1959, the introduction of painted, rolled edge, rounded corner, tin plate 'sardine can' containers became the standard.

Metal and wooden crates have standardized markings that identify the contents as to caliber, functional type, cartridge case material, quantity and cartridge/powder lot data. Specialized cartridges are further identified by a color code consisting of one or two color stripes which correspond to bullet tip color. AP cartridges with tungsten carbide cores are identified by two concentric circles instead of color stripes. Russian cartridge designation, packaging and marking practices are generally followed by former Soviet-Bloc countries; each, however, has introduced some modifications in designation and marking. Russian ammunition packaging can be distinguished from Bulgarian packaging, which also carries Cyrillic markings, primarily by the different factory codes. The factory code on the container also appears in the headstamp of the cartridges in the container.

Steel Ammo Tins
(Sardine Cans)

Wood Ammo Crate (Case)
(Contains 2 Tins + Opener)

Cartridge quantities and weights of wooden crates

Country	Manufacturer	Caliber	Rounds /Crate	Crate Weight
Czech Rep.	Sellier and Bellot	14.5 x 114	210	53 kg.
India	OFB	14.5 x 114	60	15.5 kg.
Russia	Unknown	14.5 x 114	80	23 kg.
Bulgaria	Arsenal	12.7 x 108	200	29 kg.
Bulgaria	Arsenal	12.7 x 108	200	32 kg.
Pakistan	POF	12.7 x 108	280	42 kg.
Russia	Unknown	12.7 x 108	190	29 kg.
Russia	Novosibirsk	12.7 x 108	160	25 kg.
Bulgaria	Arsenal	7.62 x 54(R)	880	25 kg.
Czech Rep.	Sellier and Bellot	7.62 x 54(R)	800	24 kg.
Russia	Novosibirsk	7.62 x 54(R)	880	26 kg.
Russia	Novosibirsk	7.62 x 54(R)	600	21 kg.
Russia	Unknown	7.62 x 54(R)	880	26 kg.
Serbia	Prvi Partizan	7.62 x 54(R)	1,200	39 kg.
Czech Rep.	Sellier and Bellot	7.62 x 39	1,200	28 kg.
Pakistan	POF	7.62 x 39	1,750	39 kg.
Russia	Barnaul	7.62 x 39	1,320	30 kg.
Serbia	Prvi Partizan	7.62 x 39	1,260	29 kg.
Sudan	STC	7.62 x 39	1,500	28.1 kg.
Ukraine	Lugansk	7.62 x 39	1,320	30 kg.
Yugoslavia	Igman Zavod	7.62 x 39	1,260	28 kg.
Yugoslavia	Igman Zavod	7.62 x 39	1,120	27.5 kg.
Russia	Unknown	5.45 x 39	2,160	29 kg.
Ukraine	Lugansk	5.45 x 39	2,160	29 kg.

Non-Standard Ammunition tin and crate marking - diagrams

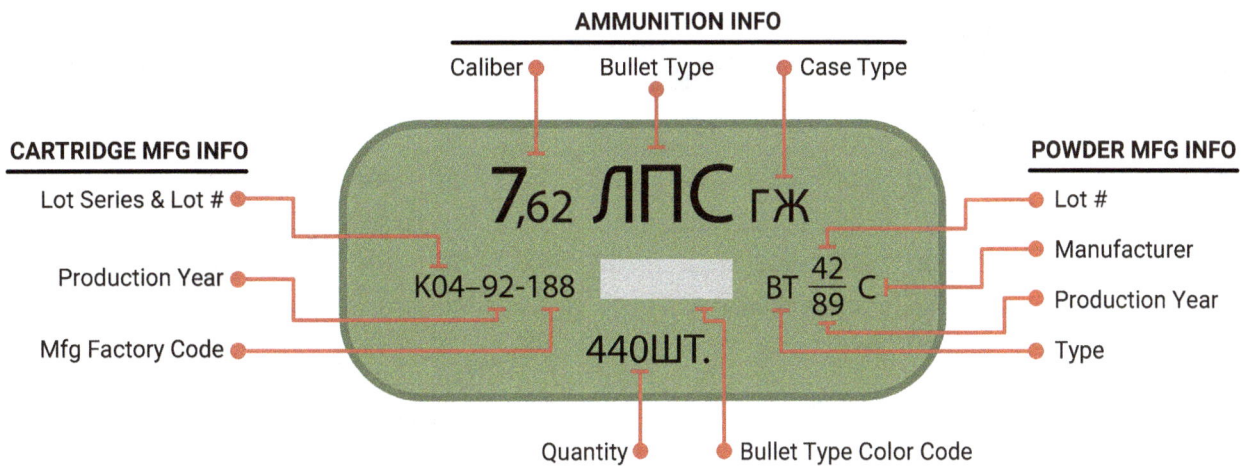

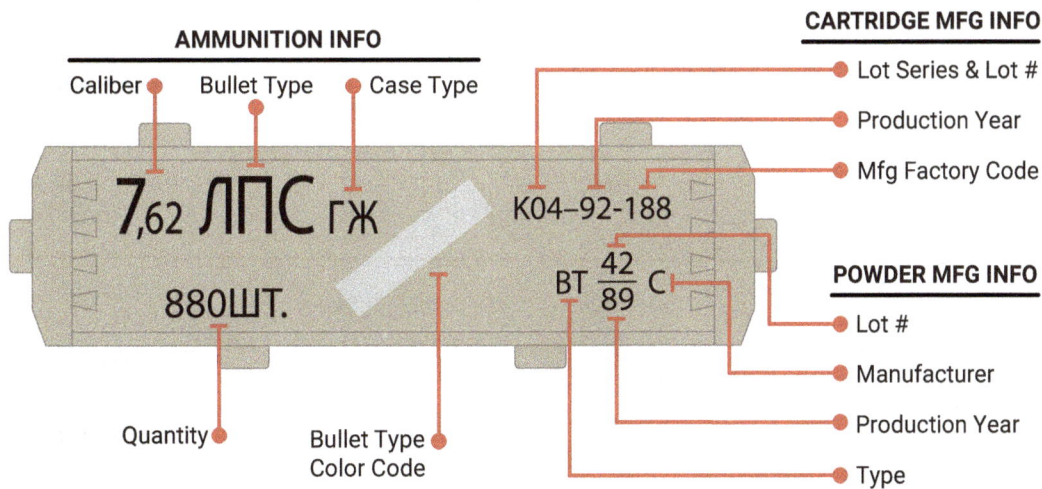

AMMUNITION INFO

Caliber ●   Bullet Type ●   Case Type ●

CARTRIDGE MFG INFO

Lot Series & Lot # ●

Production Year ●

Mfg Factory Code ●

POWDER MFG INFO

● Lot #

● Manufacturer

● Production Year

● Type

7,62 ЛПС ГЖ

K04–92–188

BT $\frac{42}{89}$ C

440ШТ.

Quantity ●   ● Bullet Type Color Code

AMMUNITION INFO

Caliber ●   Bullet Type ●   Case Type ●

CARTRIDGE MFG INFO

● Lot Series & Lot #

● Production Year

● Mfg Factory Code

7,62 ЛПС ГЖ

880ШТ.

K04–92–188

BT $\frac{42}{89}$ C

POWDER MFG INFO

● Lot #

● Manufacturer

● Production Year

● Type

Quantity ●   Bullet Type Color Code ●

Non-Standard Ammunition tin and crate marking - Russian ammunition data

CASE TYPE MARKINGS

Mark	Meaning
ГЖ	Bimetallic case (gilding metal clad steel)
ГЛ	Brass case
ГС	Steel case

CARTRIDGE MFG FACTORY CODES

Code	Location
3	Ulyanovsk
17	Barnaul
38	Yuryuzan
60	Frunze (now Bishkek)
188	Novosibirsk
270	Voroshilovgrad (now Luhansk)
304	Lugansk
539	Tula
711	Klimovsk
T	Tula

Non-Standard Ammunition tin and crate marking - Russian ammunition data

BULLET TYPE MARKINGS

Mark	Meaning
Б Б-30 Б-32 БП	Armor-piercing
Б3	Armor-piercing incendiary
Б3Т Б3Т-44	Armor-piercing incendiary tracer
БС БС-40 БС-41	Armor-piercing with special core of tungsten carbide instead of carbon steel
БСТ	Armor-piercing with tungsten carbide core with added tracer
БТ	Armor-piercing tracer
Д	Heavy (long-range) with lead core instead of carbon steel
З ЗП	Incendiary
Л	Lightweight bullet
ЛПС	Light ball bullet with mild steel core
МДЗ	High explosive incendiary
П П-41	Spotting / ranging
П3	Incendiary spotting / ranging
ПП	Enhanced penetration
ПС	Spotting / ranging with mild steel core
ПТ	Spotting / ranging tracer
СНБ	Armor-piercing sniper
Т Т-30 Т-45 Т-46	Tracer
57-У-322 57-У-323	Cartridge with higher powder charge
57-У-423	High-pressure cartridge
57-Х-322 57-Х-323 57-Х-340	Blank cartridge
57-НЕ-УЧ	Training cartridge
7Н1	Sniper bullet

BULLET TYPE COLOR CODES (Ammunition up to 14.5mm)

Color	Meaning
No color	Ball
White tip	Reference Ball
Silver tip	Light ball with steel core
Yellow tip	Heavy ball, or ball with torpedo base (on 7.62x54R)
Blue tip + white band	Short range ball 14.5x114 (only Hungarian and Czech)
Green tip + white band	Short range, tracer, (only Czech designation, only found on 7.62x39 with round nose)
Green tip	Tracer
Green tip & headstamp or entire cartridge green	Subsonic ammunition for silencer-weapons
Red tip	Spotting charge, incendiary
Red tip + white band	Short range tracer ball 14.5x114 (only Hungarian designation)
Entire bullet red	High explosive bullet (7.62x54R after 1945)
Entire bullet red	High explosive bullet (on 12.7 and 14.5mm)
Magenta tip + red band	Armor piercing incendiary tracer
Black tip + red band	Armor piercing incendiary
Black tip + red shell	Armor piercing incendiary with tungsten carbide core
Black tip + yellow band	Armor piercing incendiary Phosphorus 12.7
Black tip	Armor piercing

** The bullet tip color codes in the table above will be the same color codes on the tins or crates, but they will be color stripes on the packaging.

Example:

CARTRIDGE	TIN or CRATE
Black Tip + Red Band	Black Stripe + Red Stripe

Appendix C - Non-Standard Weapon Identification Markings

General Identification Markings

There are various identification markings found on non-standard weapons. Typically the markings will provide some or all of the following information:

- factory name or stamp (proof mark)
- caliber & serial number
- selector lever markings/symbols
- rear sight mark/symbol

NOTE: Data tables are not all inclusive, but they cover the more common weapon manufacturers.

Selector Lever Markings on Kalashnikov Rifles

Upper/ Safe Symbol	Mid/ Full-Auto Symbol	Lower/ Semi-Auto Symbol	Country
	Д	1	Albania
	L	D	Albania
	AB	ЕД	Bulgaria
	L	D	China
	进	单	China
	30	1	Czechoslovakia
	آلی	خردی	Egypt
	D	E	Egypt
	D	E	East Germany
	∞	1	Hungary
آ	ص	م	Iraq
	련	단	North Korea
	C	P	Poland
	Z	O	Poland
S	A	R	Romania
S	FA	FF	Romania
	1	3	Romania
	ЛР	ОГОНЬ	Russia
	АВ	ОД	Russia
U	R	J	Yugo/Serbia

Rear Sight Marks on Kalashnikov Rifles

Symbol	Country
D	Albania
П	Bulgaria
D	China
N	East Germany
A	Hungary
口	North Korea
S	Poland
P	Romania
П	Russia
O	Yugo/Serbia

Non-Standard Weapon Identification Markings

Factory Stamps and Countries of Manufacture

The table of symbols below are factory stamps (proof marks) for non-standard weapons. The symbols will identify the country of manufacture of the weapon. NOTE: *This is not an all inclusive list, but it covers the more common weapon manufacturers.*

⑩ Bulgaria	㉑ Bulgaria	㉕ Bulgaria	China
㊳⑥ China	△36 China	△66 China	China
Egypt	East Germany	③ East Germany	Ⓚ3 East Germany
East Germany	⓪6 East Germany	Iraq	Iraq
North Korea	North Korea	⑪ Poland	Romania
Russia	Russia	Russia	Russia
Russia	Russia	Russia	Russia
Yugoslavia/Serbia	**M.70.AB2** Yugoslavia/Serbia	ZASTAVA-KRAGUJEVAC Yugoslavia/Serbia	

Appendix D - Non-standard weapons theory overview

There are three key concepts to understand when manipulating non-standard weapons. These simple and logical concepts are:

1. CYCLE OF OPERATIONS
2. OPERATING SYSTEMS
3. LOCKING SYSTEMS

> Firearm design trends are shared across region, manufacturer and class of weapon and are relatively obvious to recognize.
>
> Keep in mind that firearms are essentially simple machines that harness the energy created by the fired cartridge to operate the system.

CYCLE OF OPERATIONS (COO)

The cycle of operations is a crucial basis for understanding how the weapon operates and for function/malfunction diagnosis. Each specific malfunction will correspond to a specific step or sometimes two in the COO. A failure in the system at a certain point, will by default, cause a failure of omission of all subsequent steps. (example – a failure to properly extract will manifest as a failure to eject.)

The COO will vary based on the type of operating and locking systems. Once the operating and locking systems of the weapon are known, the COO is logical.

The examples below all start from a standard reference point: the weapon is loaded, charged, placed on fire and the trigger is pulled.

'Cycle of Operations' Examples:

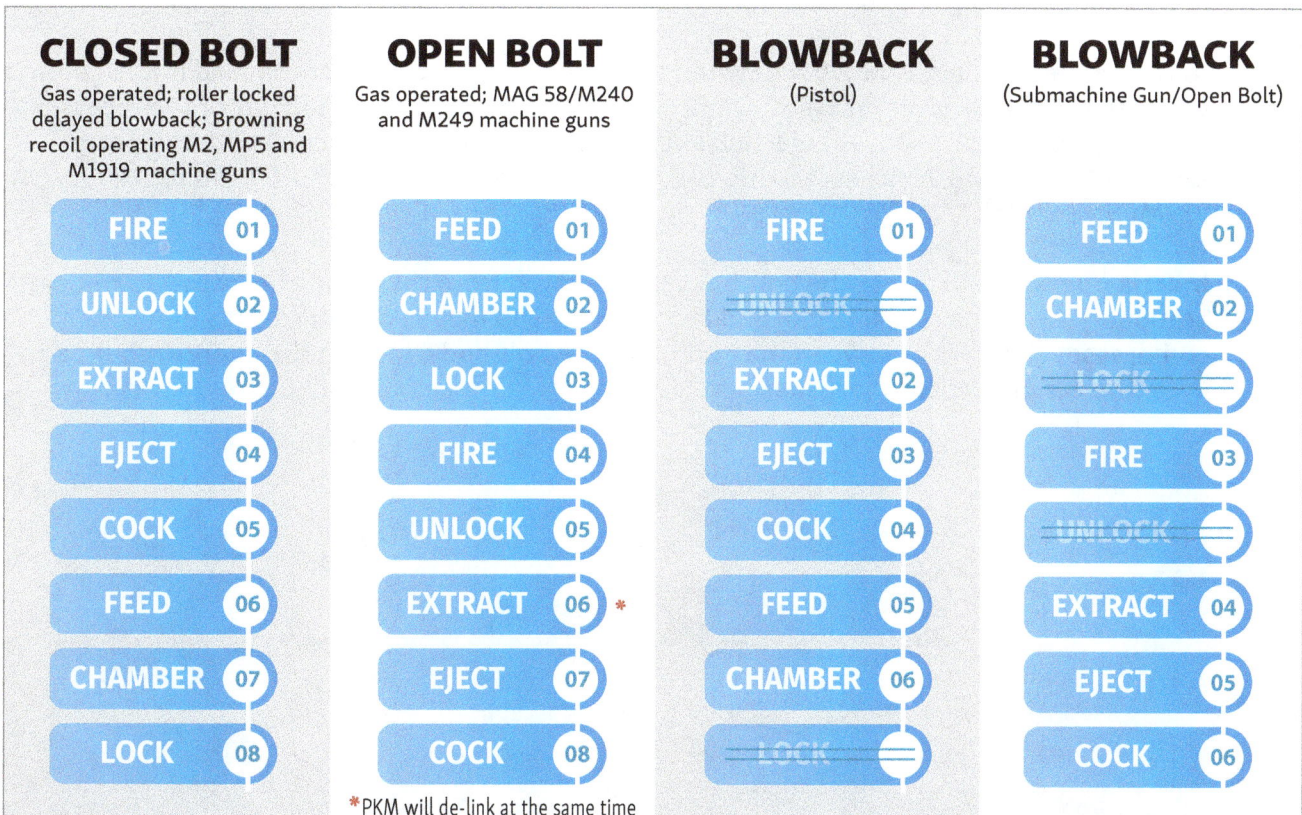

CLOSED BOLT	OPEN BOLT	BLOWBACK	BLOWBACK
Gas operated; roller locked delayed blowback; Browning recoil operating M2, MP5 and M1919 machine guns	Gas operated; MAG 58/M240 and M249 machine guns	(Pistol)	(Submachine Gun/Open Bolt)
FIRE 01	FEED 01	FIRE 01	FEED 01
UNLOCK 02	CHAMBER 02	~~UNLOCK~~	CHAMBER 02
EXTRACT 03	LOCK 03	EXTRACT 02	~~LOCK~~
EJECT 04	FIRE 04	EJECT 03	FIRE 03
COCK 05	UNLOCK 05	COCK 04	~~UNLOCK~~
FEED 06	EXTRACT 06 *	FEED 05	EXTRACT 04
CHAMBER 07	EJECT 07	CHAMBER 06	EJECT 05
LOCK 08	COCK 08	~~LOCK~~	COCK 06

*PKM will de-link at the same time

Non-standard weapons theory overview *(continued ...)*

⚙ OPERATING SYSTEMS

1. **Direct Impingement**- a type of gas operation that directs gas from a fired cartridge directly to the bolt carrier or slide assembly to cycle the action. (AR-15/M4 variants)

2. **Long-stroke piston system**- the piston is mechanically fixed to the bolt group and moves through the entire operating cycle. (AK variants)

3. **Short-stroke piston system (tappet system)**- the piston moves separately from the bolt group. It may directly push the bolt group parts as n the M1 carbine or operate through a connecting rod. (HK 416, AR180, POF, LWRC, FN FAL)

4. **Blowback**- the system of operation for self-loading firearms that obtains energy from the motion of the cartridge case as it is pushed to the rear by expanding gases created by the ignition of the propellant charge. (STEN, Makarov, M3 Grease Gun)

5. **Short recoil action**- the barrel and slide recoil only a short distance before they unlock and separate. The barrel stops quickly, and the slide continues rearward compressing the recoil spring and performing extraction, ejection and finally feeding a fresh round from the magazine in the counter recoil phase. During the last portion of its forward travel, the slide locks into the barrel and pushes the barrel back into battery. *(This is found in most handguns chambered for 9x19mm Parabellum or greater caliber. Smaller calibers, 9x18mm Makarov and below, generally use the blowback method of operation due to lower chamber pressure and associated simplicity of design.)

6. **Roller-locked, delayed-blowback**- when the bolt is closed, the rollers carried in the bolt are wedged into the receiver recesses. On firing, the rollers must be forced out of the recesses at great mechanical disadvantage, delaying the opening of the bolt, even with full power 7.62mm NATO (.308 Winchester) rifle cartridges used in the G3/HK 91 (G3, HK 91, HK 93, HK 53, MP5 variants)

7. **Inertia operated systems**- the bolt body is separated from the locked bolt body to remain stationary while the recoiling gun and locked bolt head moves rearward. This movement compresses the spring between the bolt head and bolt body, storing the energy required to cycle the action. Benelli shotguns.

Non-standard weapons theory overview *(continued ...)*

🔒 LOCKING SYSTEMS

1. **None** - all blowback pistols and some submachine guns – (STEN, UZI, M3 Grease Gun, Makarov, and CZ 82)

2. **Roller** - (HK variants, MG3, MG34, MG 42 and CZ 52)

3. **Rotating bolt** - (AK, Stoner, M60, and M249)

4. **Tilting bolt** - (SKS, FN FAL and MAG 58/M240)

5. **Tilting barrel** - (Tokarev TT33, Sig variants, M1911 variants and Glock variants)

6. **Rotating barrel** - (MAB P15, Colt All American 2000, and Beretta 8000)

7. **Locking flaps** - (RPD, DP/DPM and DShK)

8. **Falling locking block** - (P38, M9, and VZ58)

Function check
Checking the mechanical function of a weapon by replicating, without ammunition, the firing modes from the lowest rate of fire (SAFE if applicable) to the highest in a progressive sequence (not by selector location). The parts checked are the safety/safeties, sear and disconnector.

M4A1
1. Ensure the rifle is clear
2. Charge and place the weapon on SAFE
3. Attempt to fire (weapons should not FIRE, safety is functioning)
4. Place the weapon on SEMI, pull the trigger and hold it to the rear (hammer should fall, trigger/sear functioning)
5. Maintain the trigger to the rear and cycle the bolt
6. Release the trigger and listen for a metallic click (disconnector functioning)
7. Pull the trigger again and the hammer should fall
8. Charge the weapon and place on AUTO
9. Pull the trigger and hold it to the rear then cycle the bolt more than once
10. Release the trigger and pull it again, nothing should happen (auto sear is functioning)
11. Charge the weapon then pull the trigger again and the hammer should fall
12. Function check complete

Significant visual indicators
- Any checked, knurled or serrated surface
- Any movable lever or switch
- Pins with gripping surfaces
- Index marks (two lines that need to be aligned to disassembled (CZ 75)
- Recoil spring with ends of different diameters